The Courage to GRIEVE

The Courage to GRIEVE

My Story of Love, Loss, Grief, and Hope

DAVID W. INGRAM

ARCHWAY
PUBLISHING

Archway Publishing books may be ordered through booksellers or by contacting:

Archway Publishing
1663 Liberty Drive
Bloomington, IN 47403
www.archwaypublishing.com
1 (888) 242-5904

Because of the dynamic nature of the Internet, any web addresses or
links contained in this book may have changed since publication and
may no longer be valid. The views expressed in this work are solely those
of the author and do not necessarily reflect the views of the publisher,
and the publisher hereby disclaims any responsibility for them.

Any people depicted in stock imagery provided by Thinkstock are models,
and such images are being used for illustrative purposes only.
Certain stock imagery © Thinkstock.

ISBN: 978-1-4808-4160-4 (sc)
ISBN: 978-1-4808-4162-8 (hc)
ISBN: 978-1-4808-4161-1 (e)

Library of Congress Control Number: 2016921029

Print information available on the last page.

Archway Publishing rev. date: 1/9/2017

Author's Note

This book was written after my wife, Kimberly, died after a long four year struggle with cancer. I began writing a couple of short weeks after her death and finished approximately twelve months later. This is not a book only for the religious, but my faith runs through it. The information and lessons learned are for all, not just the faithful. I would only suggest that the reader believe strongly in something or someone. One can't be alone. The book is divided by topics, but the later individual chapters were often written in a journal style over the course of several months to give the reader a sense of the change in the author's tone, attitude, and emotions over the course of time. This was a year of sorrow, change, adaption, recovery, and yes, a bit of renewal. The book is mostly about grief and the slow process of recovery.

Its goal is to bring the reader from hopelessness to hope. If grief has you in a state of hopelessness and despair, please read this book and see that hope can exist again. I have included some caregiver counseling and advice on navigating the medical world. It is my hope that the reader will gain insight, but ultimately will see the great love that came out of the gift of 30 years of wonderful marriage to a great woman-- a love that still exists.

The Courage to Grieve:
My story of Love, Loss, Grief, and Hope

Is dedicated to:

My beloved

Kimberly.

Without you, I would not know love, compassion,

Nor courage.

Till the Twelfth of Never ...

ODE TO KIMBERLY--DEATH IS A FOOL

Hello Death! I see your approach.

Mark your haste tho,

For I am not done.

There is fire in me and a desire to live.

At first glance it appears your victory is clear;

I lose my family, friends, and those I hold dear.

I know you expect me to cry in despair;

Wondering Why? Surely this is not fair.

You come as if a thief in the night,

Proud of your task, and

Full of assurance that you are taking

from me all that I am.

But I tell you 'O Death that you are fooled;

For my life and my soul will not be ruled!

It is I who has played the trick on you.

You see, this body you take was not meant forever.

It was a rental really and as you can see,

It has seen better!

What you did not foresee,

That I gave my life away many years ago.

And I was promised eternity in exchange.

My future is sure. All will be well.

So you see 'O death, you are but a fool;

I go to be with the Lord. It is He who will rule.

And you are stuck with nothing but dust in the wind.

So Death, do what you must, you will not bend.

But as for me and mine, we will trust in the Lord!

I will live forever-- that is my reward!

Author: David W Ingram

Contents

Preface: Kimberly

In order to understand my thoughts and emotions while reading this book, the reader must meet Kimberly, the most loyal, kind, loving, and energetic person I have ever known.

I met Kimberly when she was a young, happy 16 years old. Kimberly was the older child, with a sibling three years her junior, Julie. She lived and was reared on Eagle Mountain Lake near Azle, Texas by her parents, Bill and Bennie Wallace. She had short brown hair that was always meticulously maintained, curled and combed, unless she was playing golf. Then it was crammed under a sun visor. With deep brown eyes that always seemed to be searching for adventure or mischief to get into, Kimberly lived her life with gusto. She had a wonderful childhood with many friends and relatives nearby. She loved the outdoors. She hunted ducks with her dad and learned to trick ski at an early age. Family trips were mostly to the Colorado mountains where hiking, Jeeping, and skiing were the norm. Her greatest love outdoors was by far, golf. She played from an early age until just months before her death.

Kimberly was small in physical stature and often overlooked by the men with whom she competed. She relished in beating them at their own games, especially golf. She also loved winning at racquetball, bowling, and just about any board game ever made.

Kimberly was a great enthusiast of any sport and could talk shop on most. If given a double dog dare, she was in.

Kimberly had many friends and loved parties and the planning of them. She enjoyed watching her friends have fun and was an awesome hostess. She never spoke ill of anyone and wouldn't tolerate those who did. She rarely had a poor disposition and was always the most upbeat person I knew. She didn't like to sit long, and was always ready to start a new adventure. She loved to travel to new places and try new things.

When I met Kimberly, I was fascinated by her perkiness and attitude. I just wanted to be around her. She had fun written all over her. After I finally talked her in to dating me at 17, we began a three year courtship that was so full of fun and excitement. Kimberly kept a daily journal back then of all of her daily activities. I found those journals a few months ago and perused them. What memories came back to me, we did so much and had so much fun! There was no doubt that we would get married someday, and we did. Thirty years later and I am writing this book. 1964 – 2015. Her life span. But the unbelievable life lived in the dash between those years was mostly with me and I am a better person because of it.

We traveled extensively as Kimberly soaked up her world. She learned as fast as she could about her surroundings and enjoyed life to the fullest. We raised a wonderful daughter, Katie, who is very much like her, thank God. Kimberly had a great career as a quality engineer at Lockheed Martin, but most of all she loved being with friends and family, sharing her love and outlook on life. She loved God and often studied her Bible with friends. She always lived by a strong moral code. She never wavered from her unconditional love of her spouse. I didn't always deserve it, but I never felt I wasn't supported and encouraged by her. She made me so much more than I ever would have been. 30 years seems like a long time, but I sure could have used 30 more. I will cherish those years and memories of the most amazing woman, friend, lover, wife, and mother.

The picture on the cover of this book is one of Kimberly as a child. I had not seen it until after her death when going through some old photos of her mother's. I was mesmerized by the melancholy mood she seemed to portray while walking through this beautiful field of flowers, the outdoors she loved so much. It seemed to foretell an early withdrawal from a life well lived. While the real emotion was probably sprung from being cajoled into slowing down long enough to take the picture by her mother, I felt compelled to place it on the cover because it so personifies Kimberly's life: a beautiful child walking through a beautiful world leaving love, compassion, and energy wherever she went and eventually leaving it way before her time.

Picture taken in July of 2013 with the "gang" in
Chicago, Kimberly is second from the left.
Also pictured left to right: Melissa Johnson, Kimberly, Jana Leming,
Nancy (Jodie) Wright, Kim Cowan, and Laura Blalock.

"Nothing is so painful to the human mind as a great and sudden change. The sun might shine, or the clouds might lour; but nothing could appear to me as it had done the day before."

Mary Shelley--Author, 1818, <u>Frankenstein</u>

Chapter 1

Shock and Awe

The large majority of the first two and a half chapters were written two weeks after Kimberly's death.

I remember April 22, 2011 the way many people remember December 7, 1941 or September 11, 2001. Not just the people who heard those events on the radio or TV reports, but those who lived on the islands or in downtown New York. These folks were so close that they knew people killed or were themselves so involved that they became a part of it. They lived and became survivors, but their lives changed so drastically, that they were never the same. They started a new path never envisioned or desired, but new just the same.

Friday, April 22, 2011 was Good Friday, the beginning of the Easter holiday and the acknowledgment that Jesus Christ died on a cross only to be raised again. This was a day of renewal and hope. By 11 a.m. that day, I was changed forever, No renewal, no hope. Kimberly had just had her first colonoscopy. She was only 46 years old and had not reached the age of 50 where one normally begins that type of exam. For her, it was already too late and there would be no early warning signs. Or had there been?

I think back now and see the signs. Oh how I wish I could go back and pay more attention, to read the hints of something going on inside of her. The first time she fell over at church while kneeling for a prayer, or the time she was so fatigued at playing only 18 holes of golf. She could play 36 without blinking. She loved the game that much. Being fatigued after only 18 holes should have been a warning sign. Or perhaps I should have noticed her new habits of crunching on ice all day long. She had always chastised me for doing that, now she was doing it almost all her waking hours. Later, I learned this was also a symptom of something happening to her body. Finally, all these symptoms told us something was amiss. She made an early appointment with her OB-GYN and had blood work done. These tests showed anemia and a high white cell count. It was scary enough that the doctor sent us straight to the colonoscopy exam. While feeling concerned, we did not panic. Surely it would just be something simple and easily overcome. A little prayer and some good-natured support from friends and we were ready to hear results. When the doctor said colon cancer, Kimberly, who normally was pretty sharp and quick to ask questions, was still a little groggy from the anesthesia and wasn't really taking it all in. I could tell by the confused look on her face and her worry at the look on my face. I can only imagine the look on my face, but I remember the moment very succinctly. It that short period of time that it took the doctor to say those two words, colon cancer, everything within me changed. A surreal moment now, those words said volumes. He assured us it was probably only Stage One and quite treatable; her colon was very clear of polyps. It was just one spot on her ascending colon that was bad. It probably had been growing there for over a year. A slow grower, he said. A few more tests and we will know for sure. Unfortunately, the pathway from Stage One to Stage Four only took a couple of MRIs. Days later, all hope was lost. The colon cancer had broken out of her colon and entered her blood stream, traveled up to her liver and tumors now existed on both lobes. Lymph nodes were involved and one of the tumors was growing very near her Vena Cava, the very large vein that travels the length of the body. If it gets into that vein, she loses her battle. At that point, the best we could hope for was a long, suffering set of treatments that might give us a small reprieve and a few years of "quality of life."

The grief I felt that Friday in April began in a burst as I cried in the arms of my friends, out of ear shot of Kimberly. I struggled to get into my truck and bring it around to the outpatient checkout. I had to get in control of myself before she got in. She didn't need to see me like this-- yet. She was still under to influence of the anesthesia and wasn't fully aware of the changes taking place in her life. But, I knew things would never be the same and the grieving had begun. The utter devastation and hopelessness that I felt at that moment was almost intolerable. I had never in my life felt so totally lost. The first of many regrets and guilty feelings began deep in my soul and the seeds of these feelings would grow more as each day turned into the next. Why didn't I see the signs? Why didn't I do my job as the protector of my family? How could I let something like this creep into my world like a thief in the night? After watching my mother and father die of cancer, shouldn't I have been more aware? Shouldn't I have seen it coming? Why? Why? Why?

C.S. Lewis, in his book, <u>A Grief Observed</u>[1] describes grief as having a similar physical feeling of that of one experiencing fear. The anxiety, disorientation, and physical body changes related to the stresses of grief and

---

[1] © C.S. Lewis, A Grief Observed 1961, Chapter 2

those of fear are very much the same. The difference is that fear is soon dissolved with an outcome and one has either overcome their fears or be overcome by them. Grief, on the other hand, can and often does, last for years and manifests itself as the changes of life causing the grief continue to change. Kimberly and I both experienced grief over the course of her four years of treatment and gradual decline into a sure death. She, now, is without grief as her soul lives with the Lord. My grief now continues, renewed in the fact that it will be suffered without her companionship. This was a new kind of grief where I wallowed in self-pity because there was no partner to stop me from it. During our grief together, we would have a day each month where we could have a "pity party." But when that day ended, it was time to drop it and "live" again. At least, as best we could under the circumstances.

Now, I wallow alone, cursed by survivor's guilt and an unquenchable thirst for answers to more questions than I have ever had, knowing that most will never be answered, at least not in this life.

Grief is actually too small a word. What I am experiencing is indescribable in that word. Imagine that a person is made up of more than just a human body and a soul, with a life span of experiences, but is much more complex. One's life is what we open our true selves to and let into our inner beliefs and convictions. We are a compilation of experiences, beliefs, emotions, motivations, and desires. All of these things rolled up into one being makes us who we are. Now, take another person, unique in their own way, but built the same with a set of experiences of their own. A set of experiences which probably caused the person to fall in love with them in the first place, like love relationships, friendships, family dramas, and disasters in the past that have created his/her personality. Blend those two separates together with deep love for one another. Let God make them one, with all these attributes boiled together toward the same goals, desires, and motivations. They become a better package; the purpose of marriage. In order to procreate and move the species forward toward a happy ending there must be a cohesive melting pot of two souls. Now, once this new single "thing" is achieved and solidifies into its oneness, let it stew for three decades and become an unbreakable, bonded by deep love, and consecrated with God's covenant a wonderful new "creation."

This creation is whole and cannot and should not be broken or divided. This is the purpose of marriage and the foundation that keeps our society functioning. Now, take this bond, and through no sin or omission, cause it to be suddenly shattered. Separate the halves from touch, communication, or consolation. Put the two halves on different planes of existence with neither knowing of the other's. Then expect one of the halves to go on living as before. Knowingly devoid of my better parts, I had to continue as if I were a whole. This is my personal definition of grief.

For others, it may be different. A child losing her mother, a sibling losing a sister, or a mother seeing a child die before she. These folks all have different definitions, but grief is still there and the grieving process must occur.

This picture of Kimberly and daughter Katie (Ingram) Drummond was taken at the Dallas Arboretum approximately six months before her death.

"Looking back on the memory of

The dance we shared 'neath the stars above

For a moment all the world was right,

How could I have known that you'd ever say goodbye."

"The Dance" sung by Garth Brooks 1990 written by Tony Arata

Chapter 2

The Beginning of the End

Sleep. What is that? I have not had a good night's sleep in so long that I can't remember what one feels like; to go to bed tired after a well spent day doing something constructive and worthwhile, like working in the field building a fence or trimming the hooves on a few goats to make them healthy. Then, I would fall immediately into guiltless slumber and re-awakening eight hours later, rested and ready for new challenges and having a bright outlook on the future. That is what I suppose a good sleep is. A pipe dream for me now, as my nights are filled with fitful nightmares and dreams of what ifs. Headaches and nausea caused by a combination of stress, poor diet, lack of exercise, and sinus congestion hamper my waking time and my sleep. My lack of a desire to take better care of myself is caused by the emptiness inside me that will not relent. I just don't care. So I dig the hole bigger with hope that I can get deep enough that the pain will ease and the demons of self-awareness will ignore me and leave me in solitude. They say there is light at the end of the tunnel. I can't even see the walls of the damn tunnel. I'm a blind man walking on the edge of a cliff who thinks he is standing in an empty parking lot. I don't even care if there is a cliff. It just doesn't matter. This is my grief.

I think of one particular recent morning. I awoke from another poor sleep after drinking heavily the night before. The memories of a nightmare still lingered. Kimberly was in need. She was always in need in the dreams, looking toward me to save her. She was begging me to help and I couldn't reach her. Now, in my waking moments, I realized the truth. I had not saved her and she was gone. I spent the morning crying in bed and not willing myself to get out. The evening would end the same way, numbing the pain with drink.

The process of grieving has many forms. Many are unseen and even unknown to the one mourning. These can manifest themselves through newly developed behaviors such as alcoholism and clinical depression or both. If not treated, these manifestations can become permanent and deadly. But at the beginning of grieving, one is not ready to build walls and put up barriers to stop these unconscious demons. They even may seem as helpers to calm the nerves and get one over the hump. I have spent many a day in a "buzz," hoping the pain would ease and let me sleep.

During Kimberly's treatment, the grief was always there. Every time the oncologist made a statement alluding to the same eventual end, and I saw the recognition on Kimberly's face, a look of despair, anger, deep sadness, and regret, such a change from her always optimistic attitude from the past. I was devastated and grieved with a heavy heart. But like a simmering pot carefully watched, it was controlled by the fact that I had a purpose, a goal, an end point. I had to "take care" of my love. I threw everything I had into this. I would show her the fight was worthy and

God would provide. Therefore the grief was manageable and I was not alone in it. We had a shared grief.

For Kimberly it was in a lost future, no grandchildren to spoil. She had already stored up a room full of clothes, toys, and baby furniture with anticipation for a great life as Grandmommy KK. There will be no future retirement with the love of her life, and no promise of good to come, only a short reprieve to suffer before an untimely death at what was supposed to be the best times in her life.

My grief was in the knowledge that Kimberly felt all these things and there wasn't a damn thing I could do about it, along with the knowledge that I would soon be alone. But at least we had each other's grief for company. Grief shared is at least on the surface easier to endure. Grief alone is fate worse than death. I think in many ways, Kimberly got the better deal. At least if the promises of God are real and true. If so, she suffers not, but rejoices in His presence. C.S. Lewis, who was reared as an atheist, but became an intellectual Christian, spoke of this and his arguments with himself over God's role in all this. He said, that if God is a good God, then our suffering on earth has a good purpose. A purpose will one day be revealed to us-- I hope. If there is no valid purpose in our suffering, then either God is not good or there is no God. Therefore, a believer must believe there is a good reason for our suffering. I cannot, because I have seen so much pain, suffering, and death in my life, see the purpose of wonderfully, innocent people suffering greatly to no good end. And now personally seeing Kimberly go through the last four years, I must question my whole concept of God and why we are here.

Don't get me wrong, I'm still a "believer," but religion as a means to get close to God seems small and archaic to me. He must be so much deeper and complex that even the most brilliant minds on this earth can't fathom our purpose. This is a task I give myself, to continue to seek God, and to understand Him wherever and whenever possible. Kimberly's suffering didn't make me question God's existence, but it did make me question our purpose in His.

Does He know my grief?

Does He care?

Does He get involved in the day to day sufferings of one of His own?

Or does He believe in a hands-off approach?

Did He just snap us into existence with a Big Bang, (A great show by the way, my only laughter over the last few months) and just sit back to watch?

Is He involved in every decision made?

I have friends on both sides of the argument. I haven't made a decision yet. The topic of God is for a later chapter. Now back to the processes of grief.

I am not a psychiatrist, but I did serve 25 years as a police officer in Fort Worth, Texas and I have seen a lot of suffering and grief -- too much really. I'm tired of it. After seeing my mother and father succumb to cancer and now Kimberly? It is too much and it is unfair. I have had enough of it and don't care to see another suffer this disease. Yet, daily people I know seem to be diagnosed with one debilitating disease or another. Is this life?

Going through a blur of time watching those you care about suffer and die? If so, then wouldn't it be better to be one of those to die than a survivor destined to watch the same story over and over again. What a pitiful mess I am. I can't decide if I want to be on the living side or not. Of course we are all on the dying side. It is just a matter of time, a dimension that gets us all eventually. So, who is to say who grieves most, those with the short time or those with the longer? Simple math deductions show that a person who lives to be 110 years old today will live through more than seven billion human deaths in his or her lifespan. Every few days I see a news story that the oldest person alive has died and they name the new oldest person alive. I think to myself, how did they get that title? Then I realize that everyone who was alive when that person was born has now died. When my daughter, Katie, was born in 1989, there were 5.2 billion humans on the planet. (Worldometers.info) If she were to win the title of oldest person, a minimum of 5.2 billion people will need to die to give her that title, including her parents, grandparents, and any other older loved ones. Today, there are over 7.4 billion human inhabitants. Look at a child and imagine how many people will die in his/her lifetime and how he/she may be affected. Kind of puts things into perspective.

Suffering and grieving seem to go hand in hand. One suffers and then one grieves, as if grieving is the continuation of suffering or a byproduct that evolves from it. If this be so, then the depth of grieving must be set by the depth of suffering, correct? The longer one suffers, the longer one grieves? If this is the case, then only a week removed from Kimberly's memorial, I have a long road of grief to travel. Must her suffering and my suffering be combined? Has her grief ended with the end of her suffering? Must I now only grieve through my own selfish, pitiful issues, or do I combine them with the four years I grieved and suffered with Kimberly? The rules here are confusing and make matters worse. I don't even know how to grieve. It isn't fair I do this without help. I am reading about grief, hence, CS Lewis and his grief story. I have my daughter, Katie, although she is in Florida trying to make a life with her new husband. I have many friends who want to help and do so whenever they can. I also have the Bible and the many verses that deal with suffering and grief. And then of course I have the great Almighty God with me as well. Then why do I feel all alone in this endeavor? Why do I crave solemnness, and silence? All of these questions make me question the purpose of my existence and make the act of religion, at least at the level I have always practiced it, seem shallow and not worthy of God's real purpose for us all.

This picture of David (author) & Kimberly Ingram was
taken as a selfie in Bath, England while celebrating their
30th wedding anniversary, August 18, 2014

"But the God of all grace, who hath called

Us onto his eternal glory by Christ Jesus,

after that ye have suffered

A while, make you perfect, stablish, strengthen, settle you."

1 Peter 5:10 KJV

Chapter 3

Suffering

Oxford dictionary defines an anal retentive as: "a person who is excessively orderly and fussy." I am an anal retentive, if you have not figured that out yet. Pedantic grousing is my norm so why not do so in grief. In order to understand a thing, I must take it apart, examine it, and then hopefully put it back together. I will take this same course with my grieving. To take my grief apart means I must go back to the precursor, suffering. I must deal with the facts of it and acknowledge the reality that it occurs and has personally occurred, often, in my life as with the deaths of those closest to me.

*

A quick note: I wrote the above one week after Kimberly's death. It is now almost three months later. My perspective may have changed somewhat, I don't know for sure. I'm not as raw but still grieving daily. Now back to the topic.

As I write this chapter, I feel the need to look in a more macro point of view in order to gain a bit of perspective. While the first two chapters were very personal and intimate, this chapter may seem a bit less so. After three months, it was time to broaden my grief view.

Suffering takes many forms; physical suffering from small pains to chronic illnesses such as depression, mental suffering from bullying to Alzheimer's, and emotional suffering from a teenage breakup to the loss of a life-long loved one. How we deal with suffering is key to how we will grieve and how we will hopefully, I'm not there yet by a long shot, recover. One of the reasons for the title of this book, The Courage to Grieve, is the realization this mandatory process is not for the weak of heart. Some succumb and some survive. I want to survive, I think. At least that is what I keep telling myself. To succumb would mean to allow the grief to swallow me up and take over. There have been many days where I have succumbed to despair and depression. I have given in by drowning my pain with alcohol and allowing my health to fail as if to flagellate myself in repentance. Now, at least most days, I feel the need to survive.

The Bible says that those that suffer will be blessed in Heaven. I hope so. There is so much suffering on this planet that Heaven is going to be the biggest rehab center ever envisioned. But what about those of us still stuck here in the muck of life? The Bible says to endure, have faith, believe. The story of Job is one of the biggest examples we are given on suffering and faith. If Job can endure, how can we not, right? Great story I guess. But I'm not sure I believe in a God who conducts lab experiments with His children to test their loyalty; a good fable perhaps? But, the moral to the story of Job is clear. We cannot fully know God. He is too vast and beyond our comprehension. We must humble ourselves and let

God be God. We must trust that there is purpose in life and suffering.

So, here we are back here on earth suffering. One way to deal with suffering is to look at "the other guy" suffering and compare his to ours'. I can't count the number of people who have said to me that they have stopped griping about their own crappy problems after watching Kimberly's struggle; a struggle that included great courage and faith. They saw things differently and now have a more thankful perspective to life and, at least for a moment in time saw the glass is at least half full. Kimberly inspired many people to refocus their lives at least temporarily. Her refusal to become a home bound invalid during her battle and continue to travel and experience life's possibilities caused some to see the need to enjoy a life that is at the best short and precarious. Their "sufferings" are not as important as they once were. They now choose to live better. So, to take my case further, should I compare my and Kimberly's suffering to something worse than four years of cancer treatments, surgeries, hospital stays, infections, days of nausea, vomiting, and generally watching the person I loved the most slowly degrade to the point that I wished her death came quicker so that she would suffer less. Compare this to the Holocaust, then maybe I can see a greater suffering. Of course I can. Millions and millions of people tortured and murdered. Innocent children slaughtered for no reason. I guess my point is, I recognize the different levels of suffering and I realize that in the grand schemes of life, my suffering is minuscule compared to so many others. If God allowed the Holocaust, then of course he is going to allow my suffering. This goes back to Lewis' point of, is there a greater purpose for all this suffering? Another group discussion class in Heaven to be scheduled, I guess. Making the statement that I realize the perspectives here does not help in my emotional state or lower the level of grief I feel. I still endure a deep loss that controls my every action. My grief is not an abstract philosophical metaphor for life;

it is as real as the Holocaust was for the world. Having perspective, though, does help me deal with anger and the, "why me?" emotions.

Now that we have put suffering into its bigger perspective, we still have to deal with our own personal sufferings. I have described myself as an anal retentive. What I mean, is I have the immediate need to fix things as soon as they go wrong. I need to dot every "i" and cross every "t" or the anxiety will keep me awake at night. A place for everything and everything in its place, now please! I feel the need to understand something newly learned immediately upon the learning of it. I use to drive my dad crazy asking him, "why?" incessantly, as a child. So, understanding the big picture helps some in the head department, especially for my type, but what about the heart department? Even now, three months later, not an hour goes by that I don't think of Kimberly.

I traveled to Colorado last week for the wedding of a dear friend. I met Katie there and we enjoyed a reunion of sorts since the funeral. We enjoyed the wedding as best we could in a beautiful setting. Imagine driving for an hour up a mountain on an old rugged, pot-holed logging road that opens up to a wide valley surrounded by mountain tops. A small lake sits between the peaks with small wooden cabins on the shore. An outdoor wedding venue has this scene as it's altar. The sun peeking in and out of clouds as dusks approaches. The bride walks down the aisle and is gorgeous, the weather perfect. The important people in my life are there. All was great, but something was missing. Something is ALWAYS missing. There is no day where I feel fulfilled, whole, or even satisfied. Everything either reminds me of Kimberly, the sound of her voice when she said, "I love you!" many times a day, her smell, she wore the same perfume for most of her life; her smile, with the one slightly crooked tooth on the left side; or, I experience something new that I immediately want to share with her. My last night in Vail, I ate at this wonderful restaurant on the patio, above Gore Creek. I had the most beautifully delicious ribeye, Kimberly's favorite cut. A small combo band was playing folk music. The wine was superb and the apple–blueberry cobbler desert was perfect and also a favorite of hers. The night was made to be a romantic evening for the two of us. The only thing missing was John Denver … and Kimberly. I found myself looking at the empty chair next to me and imaging her sitting there enjoying the evening with me. She would be wearing a plaid long sleeved shirt as it was cool and a bit rainy, probably a small jacket, also. She would have a camera and constantly taking pictures until I asked her to stop and enjoy herself. She would tell me how she loved each bite of her steak. She would ask for bread and butter and more ice tea, and even ketchup unless I stopped her first. Then when the desert came, she would fight with me over who got the most ice cream with each bite. Afterwards, she would want to find a place to dance or even run back to the room for … … Well, never mind what for. The point is, that moment occurred so vividly and does almost daily in some small way.

I talk to her as if there is a ghost in the room, but the ghost never responds. We joked before she died that she would try to communicate with me like Demi Moore in the movie, <u>Ghost</u>. I have not seen a penny move up a wall yet. This is suffering. Does it compare to the Holocaust? Of course not, but it is <u>my</u> hell on earth. It is my suffering that won't go away. Every day I try to put my suffering into the worldly perspective and realize that there is so much more, heavier, horrifying suffering going on around me. Some days it helps and some days all I can think about is, what if the world takes my daughter Katie, too. Then what? I have heard the saying, the Lord won't give you more than you could handle. Let me assure the Lord now, if he doesn't already know, I couldn't handle that. This loss of living life with a secure feeling, of feeling fragile and a moment away from utter disaster is debilitating and exacerbates the suffering. Suffering often includes the fear of "the next shoe dropping;" we are at our wits end and can't take more. A nervous breakdown is right around the corner. So we try to hunker down and avoid all of life that could harm us more. We withdraw and suffer alone and beg God to make it all go away. That is suffering.

I'm still there, but trying to force myself out of the shell now that a couple months have gone by. I am going to Costa Rica next month. I'm forcing myself to do what I really don't want to do in order to start living again. Katie has been such an inspiration to me. She feels many of the same things I do if not all of them. Her new husband, Will, has been on deployment with the Navy. She had recently moved to Florida away from loved ones, watched her mother suffer and her husband go away. She was/is alone in so many ways. And yet she gets up every day, goes to work, works side jobs, and works at church. She keeps busy and continues to live her new life. Perhaps she works so hard to blunt the pain of grief.

I am so proud of her and inspired by her bravery. Yet she continues to suffer also. Regret over moving away during her mother's illness, feelings of missing out on quality time and helping with caretaking haunt her. She has called me several times crying, and wanting to talk to her mom. She wants to discuss the things that a new wife talks to her mom about, things that I would not understand. She wants the reassurance that only a mom can give when she feels unsure of herself. Her grandmother and family friends stand in when they can, but it will never be the same. She has a hole in her heart, too.

So what is the answer to suffering? I think one must endure with hope and believe that it will get better. Seek those who understand and have empathy to what you are going through as the suffering continues. Last, a person must force himself to do things he doesn't want to do for a while, keeping one's head above water until the time when shallower waters appear. Suffering isn't easy, but many do it every day and survive. Place yourself in that group and refuse to succumb. Never say die! When the suffering finally ends, the grieving will continue, but the courageous that remain will be better prepared to grieve with a better attitude and will find solace that they have made it to a new stage as a survivor.

"Give me the gift of love.

Look me in the eyes.

Say I'm the one you're dreamin' of.

That'd be the best surprise.

Give me the gift of your sweet love

In the light of the day,

In the dark of night."[2]

---

[2] "The Gift of Love" sung by Bette Midler-1990© Songwriter(s): William E. Steinberg, Susanna Lee Hoffs, Thomas F. Kelly Copyright: Sony/ATV Tunes LLC, Steinberg Billy Music, Miranda Jasper Music

Chapter 4

Enduring Gifts

As Kimberly came closer to the end, she strove to make things easier for me. With words and deeds, she prepared the way for her own death. Her goal was never to make it easier for herself but to make it easier for me. Without my knowledge, she began buying gifts that she wanted me to have as keepsakes or things that she had heard me say I wanted in the past but had never purchased. When she was ready, she started giving me these gifts. She said she just wanted me to have them and it made her feel better.

One gift was a picture that she had taken several years before when we were in Hawaii. Kimberly, me, Katie, and Mari, one of Katie's childhood friends and a second daughter to us, were sitting together in a hammock watching a beautiful sunset on the west end of the Big Island. All of a sudden a sailboat crossed the setting sun and Kimberly quickly snapped the picture. She always had a camera in her hands and was ready at a moment's notice. The result was a curved palm tree to the right and the perfectly framed setting sun in between the sails of the boat-- nothing else. It was perfect. The memory of that wonderful moment in time was in our minds for years. Kimberly took that picture and had it placed on a piece of old wood as if it were there forever. When she gave it to me, she said I could put it up in my new home as a memory we all shared together, but since there were no faces it would be ok to keep. She believed if I kept a bunch of pictures of her around I would never stop grieving. She actually told me not to keep out lots of pictures of her in my new home. I am not sure I agree with Kimberly here. I love seeing her pictures and reflecting on the memories. However, I have tried to honor her wishes. I have kept only a few pictures of us together out in public areas.

There are many memories though, in the gifts she left for me, on display in my home.

So, here she was, doing her best to make my life after her death easier for me. Can you believe that? Her life would soon be over on earth and all she thought of was how she could make my grieving easier and quicker. We even joked about "my next wife." She was serious, but I wouldn't hear it. She wanted to make sure I married again when the time was right and that I didn't compare that wife to her. It wouldn't be fair. She wasn't even gone yet, and here she was setting the tone for something that even to this day I can't even imagine. Now I see that she was trying to put her "house" in order. She wanted to leave life on earth with as few worries as possible. She wanted to be complete. She wanted to hear the Lord say, "Come on in good and faithful servant. You have fought the good fight. You have finished the course. You have kept the faith" *(2 Timothy 4:7 ASV)*. If Kimberly didn't hear that, no one will. She showed me how to grieve even when she wasn't trying. She showed me how to live even while she was dying. She showed me how to love, even when she was coming to the end, selflessly.

Some of the other gifts she gave me were not sentimental, but just things she had heard me say I wanted at one time or another. I had my binoculars stolen several years ago and never purchased a new pair. I received a nice new set a few months before she died. I have them already packed for my trip to Costa Rica this month. She said she wanted me to take lots of trips and use them often and think of her. We both loved to travel and tried to fill her bucket list the couple years before the end. We were blessed to see much of the world in between treatments. We traveled to Costa Rica early in her treatment. She dealt with the heat, humidity, and terrain without one gripe, besting most of us in her zest to explore. There were several trips to Carlsbad, California and Las Vegas, Nevada in between surgeries and chemo treatments. We took a 15 day boat cruise down the Danube River from Budapest, Hungary to Nuremburg, Germany during which we had to do a small surgery to dig out an infected inner stitch from a recent surgery. We were literally cruising through Slovakia while I was on the phone to Fort Worth, Texas with a nurse practitioner telling me what to do. An hour later I was able to untie the infected stitch that had refused to dissolve and pull it out. The whole time Kimberly never cried out in pain, as the walls were so thin and people could here almost any sound from the next cabin. She was on only one pain killer pill. She wouldn't take too much because she didn't want to miss the wonderful dinner and view later that night. What a trooper she was! She took every step backward with courage and immediately planned a way to get forward. Our last trip was just months before she died. It was a cruise in the Baltics for our 30th anniversary. She wasn't going to miss it.

One of my goals is to live up to her expectations of me. Some might say that I shouldn't try to please someone who isn't here. I should just make myself happy and live life the way I want. My answer would be that she knew me better than anyone and she knew me better than I knew myself. Her advice is guiding me now and keeps me moving forward. There is no one in this world who wanted the best for me more than she. The good Lord gave me the best partner in life. How could I not listen to her as I go through this grieving process? I feel closer to her when I complete tasks that we talked about. I feel as if I am completing her bucket list even though she is gone. I don't know if she can see or feel my presence in any way shape or form, another mystery to be solved in Heaven, but I know that by following some of her advice, direction, and suggestions for me, my grieving is eased and *I* feel her presence. I know that eventually there will be a transition to "being my own man," making my own decisions about my future, living my "new" life. I'm just not ready yet. Thirty years of marriage, goal setting, and decisions made together as one unit takes a while to change. I feel married to her even to this day three months later. The head knows. The heart refuses to admit it, at least for now.

I have made a few head decisions. Our wedding vows said, "Till death do us part." I get it. We are parted. So I took off my wedding ring last week and packed it away with other keepsakes that will stay packed for the long term. My heart wasn't ready for it, but I thought it was a step Kimberly would want me to take in order to get the grieving along. I look at my left ring finger now and see the small indention of skin that still exists. As if an invisible ring is still there and showing the world we are still together. Maybe that is my heart waiting to finish grieving. The head will almost always get over things before the heart. Especially if I am the pragmatic, logical, analytical type as I see myself. It is important to let both parts of my body heal at its own pace. Don't push one over the other.

Another decision I made was to sell the house. This was actually a decision Kimberly and I made together and had already started the process when she took her final downturn. She wouldn't let me stop the process. She said the house was too big, and there were too many memories. She was afraid I would sit around in that big four bedroom house and mope all day while I gazed at the dozens of pictures of her around the house. She was probably right. I still was worried about the process of selling the home and going through the motions of living her final few weeks. That was a lot of stress. But her insistence and assurances kept me going. Kimberly and I wanted her to die in that house under the care of home hospice.

But that was not to be. As she continued to get weaker and the tumors in her stomach continued to grow, it became apparent that I would not be able to do what I had been doing over the last four years. I had been confidant that I could ease her pain and help her through it all, but it became apparent to me later that she had been helping me through it all so much more. Two weeks before she died, she needed to go in-house hospice for a procedure. My hope was to bring her home--for the end. But as we drove to the hospice center, she told me that she forgot to give me my last present. She told me it was in the closet, in a bag at the back corner. I told her not to worry. We would get it when we both came home. Something in her eyes told me that was not the truth.

When we got to the center, she struggled into the center with the help of a walker, but under her own power. We checked in and she ate lunch. The staff was amazed at how cogent and mobile she was. However, within 12 hours, she was completely bedridden and refusing to eat. She died within 10 days and never left that bed after that first day. To this moment, I think she decided on the way that she would not go home. She didn't want to put me through any more stress or suffering. She had decided in her own mind when and how she would die. She was headstrong and always had been. She did what she always had done. She put me before her. She put her desire to die at home behind what she believed was me struggling to make that happen.

A couple days before she died, I remembered the gift in the back of the closet. Knowing she would not return home to give it to me, I opened the gift. It was a bronze statue of a cowboy on a horse. It was entitled: <u>Trooper on The Plains</u>. The rider was a lone lawman, completing his job despite the troubles he may encounter along the way.

Foreshadowing on Kimberly's part? I don't know, but she knew I loved western art and especially Remington bronzes. When I got back to the hospice center that night, I walked up to her bed. She was at the point where she hadn't eaten for a week and was not noticeably awake. She could hear, but really didn't respond to those around her. I told her that I open the gift and loved it and that I loved her so much. She opened her eyes for just a second, gave me an ever so small smile and said, "I love you." I never heard another word from her or saw her eyes or a smile from her again. That small statue will be on my shelf until the day I die, so help me God.

Kimberly's ability to make my grieving easier, while she prepared to die gave me the best example of how to deal with not only suffering or grieving or even a poor outlook on life. The answer is to serve others first. I must live for a greater purpose than my own selfish desires. Be prepared to live life knowing that I made someone else's life better. That was the last gift she gave me. She gave me a new way to look at the world.

This picture was taken by Kimberly on vacation in Hawaii.
She had it transferred to a wood block and gave it to
her husband, David as one of several final gifts

Chapter 5

Care-giving

I was Kimberly's primary caregiver from the word <u>Go</u>. I am and have always been a take charge, "Get 'er" done kind of guy. If I was in control and "fixin'" things, I was in my element and calmed by the fact that there was a way forward. Twenty-five years as a cop with a know-it-all attitude had me prepared for this role. Devastated and grieving by the news, I was determined to "fix" it. I would make it better. I would make amends for my failure to see it coming. No one will get in my way of making things right. What an idiot, huh? But I tried. I never missed a doctor's appointment, procedure, or exam. I became an expert in medical jargon and emergency procedures. People said I could be a nurse. I had learned so much. I remembered everything important and journaled it all. (*See Kimberly's Caring Bridge journal site: <u>Caringbridge.org/</u> <u>visit/kimberlyingram</u>*™). Nothing was missed, I thought. Now, in hindsight, there are so many decisions I wish I had made differently. It was a joke really. I was never in control of anything. It was all one great big snowball rolling downhill. I tried though, I really did.

Kimberly had 50 chemo sessions. Each session would start on a Monday. For five hours, she received a multi-cocktail of deadly drugs to fight the cancer along with steroids, anti-nausea, and pain meds. Then, she was sent home with a slow drip chemo bag for the next few days, to suffer extreme nausea and flu like symptoms. We returned to the cancer center each day for fluids, and IV anti-nausea meds. While at home, there was a smorgasbord of pills. She had five different types of anti-nausea meds, four types of pain meds, two for nerve damage, shots for immune therapy, and then a litany of OTC drugs to deal with side effects of the other drugs. Constipation, diarrhea, heartburn, headaches, sleeplessness, and extreme fatigue were daily events. Drug management is a major job for a caregiver. It can easily go bad. One must stay on top of things and watch for signs of under/over dosing. Five or six doctors were giving out their own prescriptions not knowing what all she was taking. We had a color coded list of drugs that we took with us wherever we went. Anal retention is a must in this job and I had it down to a well regimented calendar of events.

The chemo bag came off on Wednesday and we returned home for the remainder of the two week period. For the next three days, I gave her shots in her stomach to help boost her immune system. Thank God for insurance. Each shot was over $7,000. Gradually over the next seven days, Kimberly would start feeling better. We would even get in a few "good" days to go to the movie or out to dinner with friends. Then we started it all over again the next Monday. Fifty times, we repeated this regime. This was between the surgeries to remove part of her colon, 55 percent of her liver, and her lower right lung. Then there was the infections, and holes in her lung that had to be operated on three times. She also had an open surgical wound that wouldn't heal, so we had a vacuum system attached that would allow her to heal from the inside out. This healing lasted seven months, a time during which she could not receive preventative chemo. When she healed from that, the tumors were back and we started all over again.

We always knew the word, terminal, would not go away, but we had hope for a long reprieve. They called it NED, No Evidence of Disease. We actually had a few months of that feeling, the feeling that we won a small victory. WE had beat cancer, at least for a while. Who knows? Others are still here. We can do this. What we didn't know was that Kimberly had developed a hole in her right lung. This was caused by the poisonous chemicals that the medical field calls cancer treatment drugs, used to slow down growth of the tumors. These drugs also made her susceptible to perforations in body tissues. It is rare they told us, though. Ha. When she started coughing up this yellow bile to the point that she could no longer take a breath between coughs, I took her to the emergency room. One set of doctors said it was just stomach acid caused by the treatments. Just take more meds. Another set of doctors wasn't sure and wanted to watch her for a while. I sat in her room while they "observed" her and watched her go into respiratory arrest. Bells and whistles start going off and "Code Blue" was yelled out the door. Minutes later, she is in Intensive Care and they want to operate immediately. I am as angry as a person can get because they ignored us initially and now I am refusing to let them operate until I talk to her oncologist and her surgeon. They both show up and still can't agree what is causing the problem. We go home to "watch" things. Months went by and things got worse until she became septic and almost died. What had happened was that a hole, a fistula, developed in the lower right lung. The lung then began sucking on bile being released into her body cavity released by her recovering liver. It had developed a bad tube as it re-grew. She was actually drowning in her own bile. Kimberly's case was written up in a medical journal because of this "rare" occurrence. There is nothing quite like making history, huh? It took five different procedures to get the proper stint in place to prevent the bile from leaking. But it was too late, the lung was mostly ruined. Kimberly would cough excessively for the remainder of her life and was always susceptible to episodes of pneumonia and infections, of which she had many. By the time she recovered from that hospital stay and she recovered from her original surgeries, the cancer had returned with more tumors -- this time in her lungs. Although Kimberly never blamed me for anything, I'll never forgive myself for not handling that episode better. I should have made more demands and asked more questions.

Now, all of the above to explain that we were spending many hours in waiting rooms, emergency rooms, doctors' offices, and hospitals. What do you find in these places? Answer: nurses, female techs, and receptionists. So to what do these ladies tune the televisions? Answer: Oprah, Wendy Williams, cooking shows, and soap operas--rarely

ESPN. I had to find ways to entertain myself. I downloaded a bunch of free eBooks. All the classics are free. I read <u>War and Peace</u> for the second time in my life. I loved <u>A Tale of Two Cities</u>, and <u>The Complete Works of Sherlock Holmes</u>. Charles Dickens and Sir Arthur Conan Doyle were great, but I found myself thinking in a seventeenth century blue collar accent. I began reading serial authors like Orson Scott Card, Vince Flynn, and John Marsden. I even took on Jane Austen. I became well read and even wrote a few things myself. I wrote Kimberly a country song, "Kimberly's Song". (See page). I became a fanatic player of a video game called, Boom Beach™. I still am to this day. It drove Kimberly crazy to see me playing this all the time, but I did whatever I could to break the boredom and monotonous waits. The iPad became my greatest friend and free Wi-Fi was a necessity. Reading large, interesting novels is also a great way to avoid the pain of reality for at least a temporary time period.

Being a caregiver means staying on top of things so that the loved one can concentrate on healing and resting.

Making sure he or she makes his or her appointments, gets a healthy diet, and takes meds when it is time. Talk to the doctors and ask the right questions because the patient is too sick to ask them. Make sure the nurses and doctors are doing the right thing. I'm not an expert in the medical field, but I know a tired overworked nurse and doctor when I see them. We all make mistakes, but there is nothing worse than a doctor who thinks he or she has all the answers and won't listen to the patient. There were times when I had to yell and make demands and other times when I should have said, "No" to things, but I didn't. But, I learned as I went along. I became stronger and more confident. No one knew Kimberly's journey like I did. They knew small parts. I knew every minute of it. I knew what had worked and what didn't. I knew the drugs that made her sick and the ones she could tolerate better than others. I knew when her vital statistics were off just by looking at her and watching for signs. I learned how to change bags full of fluids and clean open chest wounds. I have seen Kimberly's ribs and watched her scream in pain that is almost impossible to imagine. I have tried to block out some of these memories but I remember one particular example. During one of her many hospital stays, Kimberly had become septic and her lungs had drawn fluid causing severe pleurisy as her swollen lung scrapped against her still broken ribs as she tried to draw breath. A gaggle of interns were in the room trying to decide what to do. As she continued to scream in pain, I looked with anger and anguish at the lead internist and yelled,"My God! Do something! Now!" The young doctor seemed to come out of a daze as she sprung in to action and began barking orders to the nurses. Although it felt like hours, soon they had inserted a large needle into her back and drew out the fluid that was causing the pain. These types of memories still haunt me. Maybe some are best left suppressed.

I have also seen faith greater than I have ever imagined. Hope eternal, never ceasing and selfless love was her mainstay. I thought I was her caregiver, but she never stopped taking care of me. I had to keep up her hope and determination. She kept up mine. Sometimes I had to pretend that everything would be ok even though I knew it wouldn't. She pretended too, for me. I had to help her have a worthwhile life, whatever was left of it. She made sure I lived. In the four years of Kimberly's illness, in between all that I described above, we filled her bucket list. She loved to travel so we took two cruises, traveled to Florida to visit Katie and to Colorado with family. Small trips to spend at the lake with friends became small oasis from the everyday grind of treatment. The goal was to feel alive even as it slipped away. Never give up, never give in.

Some days I would confide in Kimberly and we shared our grief together, but I was careful not to wallow in it. I had others I could talk to when things got bad and they often got bad. I had a weekly lunch date with my old police partner, Harold. We could talk about anything and escape for a few hours a week. Many other friends kept in touch and still do. We were surrounded by an amazing group of friends that kept us going. I love them all dearly.

These two groups of friends we called the "Disciples," 12 of us originally, now 10, and the "Cult," the name given to the group by our daughters, euphemistically. They were/are my lifelines. A caregiver must have a support system or he/she won't survive. A word of encouragement, a small card in the mail, a meal or an errand, or a bunch of hugs and prayers, when needed, keep things going.

The hardest thing I found about being a caregiver was taking care of me. I'm still not any good at it. I retired from the police force a few months after Kimberly's diagnosis to start taking care of her full time. I just couldn't do both. While working, though, I had an exercise regime and Kimberly and I had kept pretty busy, riding bikes and playing racquetball. Now, all that had changed. My days now were filled in waiting rooms and general care taking duties for a wife who couldn't do much physically herself. We tried to walk a lot at the beginning to keep her healthy, but that didn't last as things got worse. I found myself in a depression that made my attitude so poor that I didn't care about my own health. I just couldn't get up the effort. I didn't see the reason. If my wife were dying, why should I stay healthy? I went to the doctor one time and asked for some anti-depressants to help. They helped with my attitude, but made me completely impotent. That wasn't going to work. So I compromised by drinking more and staying numb whenever I could. It didn't make my attitude any better, but the pain wasn't as sharp. So, while Katie worked long hours to keep her mind busy, exercised her body to stay healthy and helped others to keep perspective, I tried to fall apart as fast as I could. I was sedentary, slothful, and resentful of life. Katie had shown a great example for me to follow; it just took a while to see.

Sleep had become a luxury. From beeping medical equipment, midnight emergencies, extreme stress, lack of physical activity, and poor diet, sleep patterns were filled with bad dreams and constantly waking to deal with some new happening. Bandages leaked constantly and had to be changed at all hours of the day. Bodily fluids, that I couldn't imagine, leaking from many places. Kimberly was constantly apologizing that I had to do these things. Then I would feel guilty for complaining and beg her not to ever apologize to me. This was a daily routine. It never stopped. I witnessed the most independent-minded woman slowly deteriorating to the point where she couldn't use the bathroom by herself or do her own hair. She tried. Every day she would get up and do her best to put on makeup and do her hair so she would look good for me. Towards the end, this process took her a long time due to the breaks she would need to take. She would lay down on the bed for about five minutes to "get-some-air" then get back up and continue her daily routine of making herself pretty. I tried to tell her she didn't need to do that. She was beautiful to me and I didn't need her to waste valuable energy on this endeavor. But she wouldn't hear of it. It was her way of being independent and doing things for herself. The last few months, I did her hair for her and we skipped the makeup. She slowly/reluctantly gave up her attempts to do things herself. It just took too much energy. Toward the end, I did everything for her. I was ok with it. I loved her and would do anything for her, but it hurt her so much to be so dependent on anyone. It wasn't her way. It was the hardest thing to watch. Even today the memory of her slow decline and watching her lose her dignity to this disease hurts to recall. This disease took everything from Kimberly and all those around her. Not just physically, but it took her dreams and future, too. It is slow, methodical, and thorough in its ability to debilitate. It will take everything but the soul, and it will take that too if I let it. Kimberly didn't. She never lost hope or faith.

I'm doing a little better now, several months after Kimberly's death, but it was really bad for a while. They don't really tell caregivers how to do the job and take care of one's self too. Counseling on this topic is a must. Maybe I should become a caregiver trainer. I have made all the mistakes at least and could share those experiences. A caregiver must have time off every once in a while. Decompression and relaxation is necessary. Use the good friends when one can. My problem sometimes was that

Kimberly became so dependent on me that she wouldn't want me out of her presence, especially at doctors' appointments or hospital stays. Kimberly's mother, Katie, and a couple others were all that she wanted staying over at the hospitals, and a patient can never be left alone in the hospital, NEVER. I learned that the hard way. There just are not enough good nurses to go around and the tired, worn, cynical nurses just go through the bare minimum to get by. I've seen it so many times. It occurs in every profession, but is manifested so much in the medical fields where there are more needs and fewer nurses. Don't get me wrong, we met some amazing nurses that went the extra mile. Nurses Gina (never got her last name) on the fourth floor at the hospital and Angie Clark, the home health nurse for seven months, come to mind. These ladies became such good friends to Kimberly. She grew to love them and the amazingly merciful way they meticulously treated her wounds and dealt with her fears and anxieties. I will forever be in these ladies' debt. It is probably the hardest job in the world to deal with the terminally ill on a daily basis and show such compassion. A special place exists in Heaven for these folks if there is any justice at all. Kimberly had some great doctors too. Dr. Albert Yvarti whose wife was also suffering from a terminal cancer took to Kimberly and became like a dear friend to us. His reassuring ways and soft words of encouragement always made Kimberly feel better. Dr. Anwar Khurshid, her oncologist, never hesitated to deal with Kimberly's needs or return a phone call. He always guided us with a sure hand with common sense and a goal of quality of life. He never let her leave without a course of action and hope. <u>Dr. Buchanan</u>, (never got first name) was the D.O. who spent two hours sitting with us talking about Kimberly's complete history just to determine the correct drug to administer. He picked the right one. There were other great nurses and doctors that made the terrible experience bearable. But there were also those who made things worse. A caregiver has to be able to seek out the good ones and get rid of the bad. Do research, get second opinions and referrals. Be willing to say, "No" or

"We will think about it." Be insistent if it is obvious you are correct and they are wrong. Don't let the M.D. at the end of their name intimidate you. They know a lot about one thing, but a caregiver knows everything about the patient and his or her history.

Kimberly's Song
I Love Her, I Need Her

As I looked on that wall, with nothing but hope,
I couldn't believe how she called out to me;
That Daisy pump rifle with the Red Rider scope.
I got on my knees for just the right prayer:

I said to my daddy, "I love her, I need her.
I promise to take care of her.
Trust me and you will see,
She will always take care of me."

I gazed over the lot and saw the big pipes.
I could hear her motor roar out to me;
Her cherry red paint with the
black racing stripes.
I got on my knees for just the right prayer:

I said to my daddy, "I love her, I need her.
I promise to take care of her.
Trust me and you will see,
She will always take care of me."

I could hardly breathe when I knelt on one knee.
The most important question that would ever be;
Her beautiful smile and that
peach cashmere sweater.
I got on my knees for just the right prayer:

I'd said to her daddy, "I love her, I need her.
I promise to take care of her,
Trust me and you will see,
She will always take care of me."

The cancer's tough on that beautiful smile.
The pain and sufferin' is more than I can bear.
I can't do this alone, we are always a pair.
So I got on my knees, for just one more prayer:

I said to my Father, "Lord, I love
her and can't do without her.
I promised to take care of her.
Trust me, and as you can see,
She has always taken care of me."

(I wrote the above while sitting with Kimberly at the Cancer Center as she received chemo treatment number 35.)

Chapter 6

Keeping the Faith

This is a hard chapter for me. God, faith, religion, and salvation are all different words with different meanings. To understand how these helped, and continue to help me through this period of turmoil, one must realize this is a journey through many stages and continues to evolve as we go. I must start at the beginning of my faith to explain my journey. I hope the reader will have patience. And if my faith and my walk with the Lord are not a topic the reader wants to experience, then please skip this chapter. However, it does explain my and Kimberly's ability to get through this time with sane minds.

I first met Jesus on an old neighborhood mission church bus. During the summer of my seventh year, a man knocked on our door and told my mom that the local Bible church was doing summer mission work and invited nearby kids to come and have milk and donuts on the bus and hear a quick message of the Lord, so different from today where police would probably be called to investigate a guy trying to get kids on a bus. All I heard was "donuts." Homer Simpson wasn't created yet but I think he got his love of donuts from me. I guess that is why I became a cop later on. Anyway, back to the story. The old bus was parked about a block away on an unpaved side street. All of my neighborhood friends were already on the bus. Sitting inside of that old, hot and ill-equipped, airless bus, I heard a young college age guy talk about Jesus and Heaven. He explained for my seven-year-old mind how to get to this great place and all that Jesus had done to make sure we could go. After two donuts, a cold half pint of whole milk (olden days), and a Jesus story, they asked if anyone wanted to "accept Jesus." It was the first time I had ever heard the term, "to get saved." I liked the idea of going to Heaven when I died and I felt that if this Jesus had done all this for me then the least I could do was say, "Yes." Another Christian was born. Hallelujah. They, of course, invited me to attend the Bible church a few miles away on Jacksboro Hwy. The donuts would continue being served and there would be playtime. So I rode the old bus, for a few months to the Northwest Bible Church on Jacksboro Highway and started my journey. This lasted until school started in the fall. We moved to a new town a few months later and I didn't think much more about my new "faith." My family wasn't practicing religious folks at the time and we didn't really talk about God.

A few years went by and then one day another knock on the door. A youth minister from Northwest Baptist Church of Lake Worth, not to be confused with the Northwest Bible Church of earlier years, was inviting us to their church. They had decided to expand their bus service all the way out to Azle, Texas where we lived. At first it was just my brother Randy, my sister Laura, and me who went. Later, my mother would spend some time there. My father, never did, in my remembrances, attend a service or say a prayer in his lifetime. My oldest sister, Debra once told me that before he died, Dad got right with the Lord, whatever that means. Who knows? I hope so. Anyway, my journey as a Southern Baptist had begun at the ripe old age of 10.

For those who don't know what being a Texas Southern Baptist entailed in the early 1970s, let me explain. The Bible was/is the literal, inerrant Word of God. Woman wore dresses, not pants. One came to Church not just Sunday morning, but Sunday morning, Sunday night, and Wednesday night. Pot luck dinners were awesome and often. Bible instruction and in-depth study started early in life.

My first memory of Bible study was in my 4th grade Sunday school. Brother Sonny Maples started us out with the Book of Romans. One Chapter each week and we were expected to pre-read during the week and be ready. This went on all year as we continued through the New Testament. Brother Maples became my very first mentor in life. He had high standards and expected the same from each one of us. We were a pretty wild bunch and he had his hands full. He kept us all the way through junior high school level. Brother Maples was a chalk artist who, as he taught, drew the picture for that lesson. I ended up with many of those pictures throughout the years. I wish I still had them. Sonny Maples was a great man and mentor for a young boy to have. I was lucky.

The most important book for a Southern Baptist was Revelations. That was how they scared the Hell out of a sinner, literally. I remember a film they showed one Wednesday night. It portrayed different sinners throughout history going to Hell. Like the guy who had Jesus put to death, Pontius Pilate, and Adolf Hitler, one of the greatest murderers of all time. They died and burned in hell. Then they showed the average Joe dying in a motorcycle accident and not being "saved," going straight to Hell and burning right beside Hitler. Now if that didn't scare Heaven into a skeptical believer, what would?

A friend, also named David, and I were graduated to the Baptist version of an altar boy. We got to bring the flags down at the beginning of Church for the Pledge of Allegiance and then place them in their mounts and the reverse at the end of service. It was quite an honor. We always seemed to be finished in time for the noon Dallas Cowboy game. Dr. Jack Hall was a big Cowboy fan. But when it was a 3 p.m. game, he could go a little long. I remember some altar calls that would go on forever. We would sing and re-sing, "Just as I Am," until at least finally; mercifully someone would come down to that alter to be saved. Dr. Hall wasn't one to give in lightly. This was my childhood Christian experience.

When my High School years began, I stopped going to Church. I don't really remember why other than life got real busy and I got a little wild. That's a topic for another day. I did keep reading my Bible and prayed daily. This never stopped. One can take the Southern Baptist out of a Church but you can't take Church out of a Southern Baptist.

As I said before I was a wild child for a few years there early in high school. I'll leave out the sordid details, but suffice it to say when I met Kimberly at 17, things changed. We began dating and she invited me to her Church, The First United Methodist Church of Azle. In the early 80s, there were few teenagers in the church. It was gentrified and local kids from Azle were not there. And to be honest, coming from a fire-and-brimstone Southern Baptist upbringing, I could see why. Boring was a nice word. Also monotonous, scripted, and unemotional come to mind. No fire, no brimstone, and no Revelations. At least the Church of Christ across the highway sang interesting music even though they didn't have a band. At least the preacher could get down and crazy when he wanted to. I had a girlfriend once who took me there. I could dig it, but not this hifalutin' stuff.

Well, to make a long story short, we got married by the Methodist reverend and became members of the First United Methodist Church of Hurst. I spent the next 15 years in that Church. We met a group of friends that 30 years later had turned into the "Disciples." A group of friends that make life worth living and have given me hope that everything will be ok--those kinds of friends.

I was determined to expose these Methodist children to a little Southern Baptists' style of teaching. I taught third, fourth, and sixth grade Sunday school classes. Sixth grade was "confirmation" year where the child made a confession of faith. What I called being, "saved." Anyway, I tried to be what Brother Maples would want me to be in my foreign environment. We were all Christians, right, just a different style, music, and façade? I enjoyed teaching the Gospel to the children and mentored as many as I could. The only problem I can recall of that time was when a certain precocious little third grader asked if Santa Clause was real, right in the middle of my lesson. The ramifications from that day haunted me for years.

We tried other styles of worship over the years too, Lutheran via De Cristo, even a little Pentecostal style Holy Rollers. Kimberly and I had walked our faith together since we were 17 and she had grown much as a Christian over the years. She had even gotten baptized with Katie as an adult. You know, the full dunk, like a good Baptist should. She was always curious about the Bible. She didn't have the in-depth study of it as a child like I had, so she was always hungry to learn more. We spent many nights just going over scripture and what it meant to us and how to interpret different passages. We did adult Bible studies and learned as a family. Kimberly never stopped studying and growing as a Christian. She read and marked up her Bible, (now a precious possession of mine) highlighting her favorite passages. Her faith never wavered--ever. During the four years of her illness, Kimberly and I had many long conversations about death, dying, Heaven, and God in general. She had always wanted to learn and grow in her faith but now she had urgency. She was so anxious to grow her knowledge of the Bible. In the past, Bible study and faith were ethereal and philosophical. Now it was practical and topical for the future was at hand. She wasn't just looking to learn, she was learning to understand what was soon to come. We spent many a conversation talking about what life after death would be like for us.

She often wondered when things would happen to her and would she know others. I remember one day when she asked me, "Will I know who you are? Will I see my Granddad when I get there?" I discussed with her the story in Luke, when Jesus was on the cross and the two criminals were on either side of him. One ridiculed Jesus and the other recognized who Jesus really was and asked Jesus to remember him. Jesus told the criminal that before the day was over he would be with him in his Kingdom. Kimberly felt very comforted by that story, and as we discussed Jesus' talks about his Kingdom and how he went before us to, "prepare a place for us," she was content to know that she would be in a good place. I know Kimberly had the normal fear of dying and what she would miss on earth. We discussed those things too, but there was never a doubt in her mind, or mine, that she would be in Heaven. Her faith had eased her walk through this disease because she knew that we don't really belong here and our bodies are all flawed and decaying. She knew that her future with the Lord was where she truly belonged.

One of these many discussions with Kimberly led me to write the poem, "Death is a Fool," in her honor. We had just had a long discussion and she told me she wasn't worried about death anymore and she wasn't scared to go. I was taking a shower (a great place to think) later and the words came to me then. After I wrote the poem, I read it to Kimberly and she said, "Yes, that's how I feel." I had it placed on Kimberly's memorial service program. (See introduction.)

People might assume that my present attitude about religion came because of Kimberly's plight and "failure" to be healed. Not true. I never lost my faith or the roots of my beliefs, but I did lose my belief in the practice of religion. I had gotten involved, unfortunately, in church politics and committees years before Kimberly's illness. This led to seeing the underbelly of religion. It wasn't very pretty. For years I have seen preachers give Zig Ziglar-type sermons that are great little pick-me-uppers for the coming week, but actually say nothing about what was really going on in the world. They didn't take a stand on anything important when so much was happening in our world that needed leadership from a faithful preacher. We even went back to the "Baptists," looking for something real. I put the word in quotes because they mostly don't use the word anymore. It scares away the middle-of-the-roaders, the newbies who don't like fundamentalism, what I grew up on. Now they use cute universal names for churches that include anything and anybody, like "The Community Church," or "The Corner Church," They have coffee shops inside, but often no cross outside. We don't want to offend, do we? The preachers, most of them, stay away from controversial topics and instead quote Old Testament stories and stuff out of Psalms that won't offend anyone, *the money*. I stopped going to Church. I was finished. I had heard it all. I felt that religion had let me down. But not Kimberly, she still craved it and she loved a good Baptist-type sermon. I guess because she didn't grow up on it like I had, she still craved it and saw it as new.

So, this is where I was in my faith journey in 2011 when Kimberly was diagnosed with cancer--a cynical, angry Christian, still believing in God, but not the Church that was to deliver his message.

I actually was at church with Kimberly the first time she fell over with early symptoms of extreme fatigue and anemia from the cancer. We didn't know what caused her to fall at the time. We thought she was sick with sinus infections as had happened yearly with her for as long as I can remember. She went down one Sunday to pray at the altar. When she tried to stand afterwards, she fell over. She almost passed out. She was very embarrassed as we walked out. A couple weeks later we got the diagnosis. I never went back to that church. It is hard to say why really. I guess in some subconscious way I blamed God, and that church, for not catching the cancer early and healing her at its onset. Sounds silly I know, but when your old faith gets tested, a lot of weird things start coming to mind. I went a few other times to Katie's church over the next few years during Kimberly's illness but I couldn't get into it. I was really mad at the world by this time and hearing the same old fluff over and over again wasn't helping.

I prayed though. Man I prayed, daily, hourly, minute by minute sometimes. I wanted God to know I wasn't mad at him, just religion as an institution. Please don't let this affect Kimberly or her health, I prayed. My cynicism shouldn't be held against her, surely not. At this point, at the beginning of her diagnosis, all my faith revolved around believing that God would take care of us; our faith was solid.

We prayed, and so did everyone else. I received an email from a Catholic friend that over 3,000 nuns were praying for Kimberly. We were on so many prayer lists that there had to be a hundred thousand prayers going up daily. How could God not hear our pleas? Our Christian friends gave Kimberly prayer boxes, embroidered verses, daily devotionals, and spoke of large prayer gatherings where Kimberly's name had been lifted up. How could all of that not lead to a miracle healing? Does God really want Kimberly to go through this living Hell on Earth? How does a cynical, old, heard-it-all Christian deal with personal tragedy and stay a believer? A good question, I'll let you know how it ends someday.

The next few years would bring a lot of new and different thoughts, questions, and perspectives toward God and his purpose for me. My faith and our marriage grew during this time though. My prayers became more personal and specific and I tried to open my mind to different forms of healing. At first I prayed for physical healing, just like everyone else. Eventually though, I came to realize that our earthly bodies aren't God's focus. Jesus healed to prove who he was, but he always told why he was there, to heal our souls and bring us into his Kingdom. I began to pray for spiritual healing and contentment. I prayed for God to take away some of my burdens or at least make me strong enough to endure them. I prayed for my marriage and relationship with my family. We did feel the presence of God in our lives every day through the outpouring of love from friends and family.

The last four years of our 30 years of marriage was by far the most enriching. Why? Because we became selfless toward each other. We left the pettiness that sometimes gets in the way behind us and began living each day as it could be the last, because we knew it could be. We took in all that was around us and enjoyed our friends and family as if they were new to us. We began looking for the little gold nuggets of life that God leaves laying around, small moments in time that define who we are and want to be. Moments of calm beauty in a life of turmoil became an oasis to us. Sometimes we would sit on the porch and watch the sunset and say nothing, reveling in being together. The two little girls from across the street, Evynn and Grier, would come over and give Kimberly hugs and lift her spirits.

Sometimes the moments would be seen in the beautiful places we traveled to and sometimes just in fellowship with our friends and family, but we never stopped looking for them. Even to the end Kimberly strove to see the beauty in life. Those moments were healing for us. We felt God's touch on us through it all. We were so thankful for the 30 years of marriage, but most thankful for the last four. We felt like we had finally obtained the goal all marriages strive, to be one. The prayers worked and we were healed.

Now, some might say that God created all this to bring us to a greater, more profound relationship with him. I see it that God saw life happening as it often does, and then took the opportunity to show His presence with grace and mercy. He didn't cause the bad; He took advantage of it to make a point. Could this be what really happened to Job?

When Kimberly was finally overcome by the cancer, she couldn't stand alone or even brush her teeth. We knew what was coming and we prepared for the end. Kimberly told me her bucket was full and she felt so blessed by what God had given her in her life. Her only regret was leaving her loved ones, but she was secure in the belief that she would see us all again. She made a few videos saying, "I'll see you again." She even made some for her unborn grandchildren. The videos were little talks about things that would happen to them as they grew up. Topics included: enjoying Christmas correctly, driving for the first time, and dating. It was important to Kimberly that her grandchildren would know her and hear from her. She wanted to have influence on their lives. At the end, she was confident that she had said what needed to be said to everyone. She had lived well, loved well, and served well. She didn't go quietly into the night, but she went knowing she was loved by many and led by a God of grace and mercy. When she took her last breath, I didn't see her soul ascend into Heaven, but I had no doubt that it did.

When Kimberly died, three months ago now, I was at peace with God, even though I had a lot of questions. I greatly appreciate all that He gave us in our lives and marriage. I don't blame God for cancer taking my mother, my father, and now my wife. Life happens to us all. Kimberly lived for 50 years and enjoyed the large majority of it with gusto and pleasure. I was blessed to be a part of it for 33 of those years. I got to be her best friend and lover. I will always be in the Lord's debt for that gift.

So, for the most part, I feel blessed to have had the last 33 years. The future? I am alone now and I still seek contentment. It seems to elude me wherever I go. I am still in that mode of transition, seeking answers and direction; finding some, but others remain. Right now, I'm still in the phase of working things out in my head and my heart. I know that I believe in God the Father, the Son, and the Holy Spirit. I know that God, in whatever form, is Love in its purest form. I know that God hears my prayers and suffers with me in some way, just as He did when Jesus hung on the cross. I know there is a Heaven and that Kimberly is there in some form, unable to communicate with me but able to communicate with God. I'll take that for now. Everything else is up in the air.

At the beginning of things, the questions came at me daily. Most of them began with why? Why the suffering? Why aren't some prayers answered and some are? Why did my Love that You, God, gave me have to suffer for four long years and deteriorate to nothing? Why didn't her prayers get answered? Why? Why? Damn it! Why? Don't give me the crap that, "It is God's will," or that "God must have wanted it that way." I swear if I hear that one more time I will slap the person who says it. Do not tell me that the God of love, mercy and grace wills for any child of His to suffer. Do not tell me that her death served a greater purpose or that her time was done. I'm sorry but I will call *Bullshit* on that. Anyone who says these things may mean well, but they have not lived it. They just spout stuff they have heard. I don't blame them really. What do you say? Sometimes it is best to say nothing at all. Listening is definitely a gift from God. I wish I had a better grasp of it. I recall that Job's friends messed up pretty good when they started giving their opinions too quickly.

What I believe now is not what I believed in my past, and will probably not be what I believe in my future. Like I said, it is a journey. But, what I believe today is that God allows suffering because of free will, the need to let us choose to love him on our own accord. Real love, not rote worship in order to, "Get to Heaven" is what he wants from us. The byproduct of free will is our own ignorance and mistakes (sin). Does cancer come from our mistakes in the world? Bad diet, poor habits, bad genes from a gene pool poorly maintained? Probably. I believe that God doesn't interfere with most of what happens in the world unless what happens gets in the way of His overall plans for the world. Then He sticks a finger in here and there to get it in the right direction again. I believe He answers prayers in ways that we can't imagine, but that prayers for healing our bodies and other earthly body functions are akin to prayers for the Cowboys to win on Sunday. They make for a good prayer, but do they serve the greater purpose? My apologies to those that believe the hole in the stadium was built so that God could watch the game. I believe if we truly have the Holy Spirit in our hearts that our prayers are answered in some way. Some comfort is obtainable, some good is shown to us; some future pathway is observable if we are open minded to "see" what is placed before us. I know that my faith, and Kimberly's faith, and Katie's faith have helped us get through some of the worst days of our lives. Days where pain and anguish left us with only one last action to take, pray. My belief in an eternal life beyond these much flawed bodies and this much flawed Earth guides me to continue to search for God wherever I go. I don't have all my answers and may never get them, at least not here on this rock. Who knows though? I still have the big rehab center in the sky to look forward to.

This chapter is about where I am now and how my faith helped me get through these last few years; how I have evolved and continue to evolve. This chapter is not meant to be preachy or even a guide to what is right or wrong in religion. I'm not an expert by any means, but I know that I will keep learning and searching. I would love to say that I am a perfect Christian, whatever that means, but I am extremely flawed in so many ways. I have not been as good an example as Brother Maples was to me, and I have not mentored near as many young people as I would have liked. But the few with whom I have been able to spend time, and be an example to, and keep up with over the years, have turned out pretty well. Hopefully, some of my lessons and mistakes have taught them to be better people. My life is not over yet and I hope to do better and live by the examples Kimberly has left for me. She will remain alive in me, and in Katie, and in the people she has touched over the years. God worked much in her short life. That is how I see God working through all this with me. Through her examples, deeds, deep undivided love and devotion to our marriage, I will be a better person. A day doesn't go by that I don't think of what she would say or do in certain situations. She is very much alive in my life. My walk of faith will continue and I don't know where it will lead in the end, but to Heaven and the Lord, and where Kimberly awaits. Everything else is fluff.

❁

Six months have transpired since I wrote the above portion of this chapter. I have continued my search and study to determine, WHY? The more I learn, the more I realized I don't know and the more questions arise. The one thing I always come away with is that God is so much bigger than we give Him credit for. We are so quick to place God in a small Earth-sized jar and keep Him understandable to our small minds. I am learning to open my mind to many possibilities and aspects that mainstream religions discourage. Being a Christian to me means so much more than we are often taught on a superficial level. I am definitely on a journey of discovery that I know will never end. At least not until I see Kimberly again.

❋

There is one last topic on the faithful before I end this subject. If the reader is religious then he or she probably has many religious friends and acquaintances. You must be ready for the following: "He/She is in a better place," or "You know they are still with us in spirit," or my least favorite, "It is God's will." That last one almost sent me into outer space once. My point is that people often don't know what to say and when they do say something, they try to give comfort as best they can with what they think someone suffering wants or needs to hear. They mean well and that is the way I have always taken the little words of wisdom. Let me assure the world though, I never felt Kimberly was in a better place, and if she is, why the heck am I stuck alone in this crappy world? I never felt her spirit hovering around me keeping me company, she is gone and she isn't coming back in this lifetime; consequently, I certainly don't think her death was God's will. He might have allowed it to happen, but willed it to be so? No. Christians and people of other faiths rely on and hope on the fact that there is life after death and I certainly believe this also. However, soon after a tragic death of a young person, hearing these little platitudes never helped me. They often made me angry and seemed to simplify a very difficult and complicated set of circumstances that ultimately ended the better part of my life and history. The grieving shouldn't feel guilty for having these feelings and the anger that comes with it. Time will help with this and give perspective many months later after some pain has lifted. Faithful helpers should not be upset that the grievers that they are trying to comfort are not comforted by words. Be patient and let the grief work its course. They haven't lost faith, they are just angry. God knows and is aware and will not leave them. He also suffers from our pain. This kind of tragedy often makes a person question his or her faith and the strength of the bond with God, but it often can be a stronger bind in the end. There is nothing quite like suffering and adversity to make a person look deeply within to see what he or she really believes in. The end result may very well place the person way past where he or she could have gone otherwise in his or her walk with God. Hopelessness can become hope once again. I did it with God's help!

"..And friends are friends forever

If the Lord's the Lord of them

And a friend will not say never

'Cause the welcome will not end

Though it's hard to let you go

In the Father's hands we know

That a lifetime's not too long

To live as friends."

"Friends" sung by Michael W. Smith- 1983© lyrics by Debbie K. Davis

Chapter 7

Playing Well with Others

As I have said previously, I am a take-charge, do-it-myself kind of guy. Taking care of Kimberly became my one and only job and I was determined to do it better than anyone else could. I didn't want help from anyone and no one was going to tell me how to do anything. What an idiot! Have I said that yet? It is amazing how adversity makes you wake up and see your little, and large flaws. I had gone through most of my life, 46 years of age at D Day, (D stands for diagnosis) thinking I was smarter than most people in the room and didn't need anyone telling me how to do it, whatever it is. I also felt most comfortable when I was in charge and on top of things. I began by taking the same pathway toward being Kimberly's caregiver. Do the research. Learn all I could quickly. Make a plan. And, then execute said plan--easy peasy. Well, we all know what they say about plans? They last until the mission start and then everything goes to heck. My first mistake was thinking I could keep working my nine-to-five job and take care of Kimberly part time. It just wasn't possible. I know some do it out of necessity and I really feel for those people. There are just too many things that have to be done from nine to five, like all doctor's appointments and most medical procedures. I was lucky in that I was able to retire at an early age. Fort Worth had a 25-year retirement for Police and Fire. I had just passed those 25 years. It was time to go and be a full time caregiver. It was tough to give up being a cop and the feeling of accomplishment that comes from helping your community, but now there was to be just one focus and that was my new mission -- to take care of my wife.

My second mistake and biggest had more to do with my personality trait that made me a good leader as a cop, and that was to take charge and get it done ASAP without emotion. To get the job done as a cop, I had to put up walls. The walls protect us from seeing the nitty gritty dirty side of life and then internalizing it. It keeps cops from committing suicide. Civilians see our words and behavior as a warped sense of humor or at best a macabre outlook. I remember one call I was on in particular that illustrates this well. There was a fatality accident on the freeway. An Alzheimer's patient had walked out of a home and began walking across this busy highway. A large Cadillac hit her at about 75 mph. When I pulled up on the scene, I parked a little bit south of the main accident area to let the oncoming traffic see my reds and blues and maybe slow down a bit. As I began walking up to the accident, I began feeling something soft and squishy under my feet. I looked down with my flashlight and saw what looked like pieces of raw chicken lying on the road. At this point, an ambulance driver came walking towards me carrying an empty Budweiser 12-pack carton. He approached me and I asked him what was all over the road that looked like chicken pieces? He said, "The car hit her so hard that she exploded. Now I gotta pick up all the parts. You know what they say about chicken? Parts is parts." Now the average citizen hearing that and seeing a human being picked up in a discarded beer carton would be outraged and disgusted. I just laughed and told him, "Good luck finding the wishbone." Even now, telling this story, I feel really guilty; but the story has to be put in to proper context. When one sees things like this every day, even worse things that I won't mention; it can eat at an officer and destroy him/her if he or she lets it. One has to develop a gallows humor and build walls to emotions that these memories can't get to. That's how I lasted 25 years. I have known a couple officers and one friend who didn't, and they "ate their guns."

This was how I was going to attack the new job as caregiver. It didn't work out so well. First, I was already way too emotionally attached to Kimberly and there was no detaching from the situation. Secondly, it was the same tragic scene every day; pain and suffering every day, watching my loved one deteriorate every day. I put the emotions away to "protect" her, I thought. But Kimberly was very aware of how I was affected. We were so connected in every way; we felt each other's pain and emotion. Our pity-party days were the only way we could deal with things. After that day, each month we put away the pity and tears and pressed on. To quote Andrew Dufresne from The Shawshank Redemption, "You gotta get busy livin' or get busy dyin'."

We chose to live, but there were days that the pressure seemed too much to handle. Over time, the stress took its toll and physical damage to my body occurred. Headaches, ulcers, reduced immunity to sickness, and general depression all set in at different times. As much as I wanted to do everything myself, I had to let family and friends in to take some pressure, Kimberly knew this and did not argue when I needed the breaks. I know she wanted me there at all times, but I just couldn't be. Katie, her mother, my sister, her sister, and several friends all took turns overnight at hospitals and at chemo centers from time to time.

I had to be more like a Marine; willing to improvise, adapt, and overcome. The key, I found out to this strategy is to let the people in who want into the inner circle. I had to trust friends and family to help me and serve me, even though I did not want to be seen as helpless. There were so many days that my brain was fried and I was so exhausted that I couldn't think straight enough to help myself, much less Kimberly. If it weren't for family and close friends, I wouldn't have made it. I learned all of this the hard way, by driving myself to stress-related illnesses and near to a nervous breakdown. I came very close a few times to going crazy, but those around me saw the needs and took up the slack when and where they could. Many people brought food to freeze and bring out later after a long day at the clinic. Some sent gift cards to restaurants that were quick and easy to access. Some sent weekly cards of assurance and hope. Some made beautiful spiritual prayer blankets and other items with scripture. All of these things were helpful and showed the support that kept us going when things got tough.

Communication was a major issue. When you have so many people always wanting to know the latest doctor report or scan results, phones can ring off the hook. We chose instead to appoint one person from each friend or family group to be responsible to inform the rest of the group. I would send out one group message to about four or five folks and they would take care of it from there.

Another resource that was extremely helpful was a webpage called, CaringBridge.org™. On this free site, we began a journal from day one. Any interested person could sign in and follow along with Kimberly's progress and then leave words of encouragement. It also allowed for a permanent record of events. Many times, I would go back to that journal to remember dates of procedures and operations as the years went by. That journal is still available online and there were almost 25,000 hits on it last I looked.

When it comes to communicating things to others it is best to find the few people one can trust and assign them the job of being the "Chief Communicating Officer."

People know who they are and call them, not you. It takes a lot of stress off. So many people want to help and don't know how. Many of these people are type A personalities and all they need is a set of instructions and a direction to go. Once released to their jobs, they take care of business. Not only does this take a load off the caregiver, but it really allows those who want to be a part of the caregiving to feel useful. Don't feel like you are taking advantage of them. They will actually feel thankful for being given a useful purpose. There is nothing worse than feeling helpless as a friend or family member suffers, and it isn't just the caregiver feeling that way. As primary caregivers, we must include those directly around us as much as we can and as much as they are willing. Those who aren't really serious will quickly move away, but those who seriously want to give their time and love to help become instant relief and comfort. I didn't do as well as I should have in this area and I paid the price.

One lesson I did learn about these secondary caregivers occurred after Kimberly died. They didn't go away. They stayed and tried to take care of me too. In reality that is what they had been doing all along, taking care of both of us. It just became obvious after Kimberly died. I still get calls and visits. I get dinner invites so often that I'm gaining weight. There are so many wonderful people who care and just want an opportunity to show it and all we had to do is pay attention to the folks around us.

On another topic of dealing with those around the griever is what I call, "wearing two faces" or "having two voices." I remember my mother doing it when I was a kid. She would be yelling at us kids with her I'm-about-to-kill-you-all voice, then the phone would ring and she would answer it with her sweet-as-molasses voice. She would finish her conversation sounding as if there wasn't a care in the world, hang-up, and finish us off in her kill-you voice as if there were never an interruption. As a griever this last year, I have had many opportunities to use several voices and faces around a lot of concerned people. When they ask, "How are you doing?" There is an opportunity to tell them the truth which will put a damper on things or I could put on a face and voice that says, "I'm good." Picking the right time to do either is sometimes hard. Those really close to me probably did want to know how I was doing and knew that life sucked and for now and had stopped asking. Those who didn't see me often and did not know how I was doing may really have cared but I did not want to bring them down by giving a sob story that everyone already knew. After a while, the sob stories even begin to bore me. Who wants to hear that life sucks all the time? For those whom I only know casually, I put on the face and I am as uplifting as I can be. You never know when their day already sucks enough. I don't want to add to the burdens of their lives.

Now, this is not to say that a person in this vulnerable place shouldn't have a confidant, someone whom I could tell everything and they never complain that I was burdening them. I have several and they keep me honest about my feelings. This was very important that I was able to be honest about my emotional state and receive the support I needed. The right friend can keep one on the edge from going over. As you begin to come out of your funk; however long that may take, you begin to see the light at the end of the tunnel, don't forget to share that with others. They need to celebrate with you as you recover. It is only fair that they get some reward. They have suffered too.

My final thought on this subject is just a bit of advice for caregivers. It is an important job but we are not Supermen, but there are lots of super men and women in your sphere. Let them in. In the end, you will be healthier and possess such a healing force that will surround you in your times of need. These people will be life-long friends and connections. Just give a little trust to them and they will not fail you. Kimberly and I have been so blessed by these people and they have been a major part of our godly healing. There are so many Thank Yous owed and yet none are expected. My only worry is that when I am needed some day, will I be there for them like they were there for me?

"Now that I'm on my own?

What we did together

Beats anything I've done alone.

Since the day that you left,

I've been asking myself,

Is this how it's gonna be?

Without you,

What do I do with me?" [3]

[3] **Song by Tanya Tucker (Without You, What do I do with Me?) 1991©**
Written by David Chamberlain, L. David Lewis, Royce Porter

Chapter 8

Making the Transitions

This chapter and the next two are written in journal format over time. As they were written, often at the same times, there exists a blend of experiences even though the topic is different. The purpose of this style is to give the reader a sense of the changes occurring with me as time goes by.

August 30, 2015, As I begin this chapter, I am sitting on an airplane returning to Texas after a month long trip to Costa Rica. Why? Why not? I have just sold our home, packed everything away or gave it away. I am fully liquidated with nothing to do and nowhere to go. My caregiver job is over. My one daughter is in Florida waiting for her husband to come back from deployment. My new apartment was not ready for me to move into. So I went to a place I loved for a little solitude and thinking space. I got a condo on the beach in a secluded neighborhood called Playa Flamingo. The first two weeks I did little more than read and write and watch TV. I read C.S. Lewis' science fiction trilogy. I wrote chapters four through six of this book, and watched a lot of Spanish language TV, (a great way to learn Spanish by the way). I sat on the deck and listened to the surf and drank beer while listening to my iPad music. I rarely observed English speakers and very few Spanish speakers. I was very alone. I felt that I needed the time to think and work through some necessary transitions coming up in my life. Part of these transitions dealt with moving and deciding where to move, and part of them were emotional transitions.

At the time of writing this chapter, I'm almost four months from Kimberly's funeral. Her headstone has not yet been delivered. Things are still very raw and fresh in my mind. Our 31st wedding anniversary passed last week. Luckily, a good friend of mine, Mike, came down beginning in week three and spent the last two weeks with me. It was a good change from the two weeks of solitude. We traveled the country, took tours and drank a lot of Imperial Silvers on the beach. Mike really helped me through this time. Mike has the perfect loving, understanding personality for my situation. We have similar outlooks on life and he helped to keep me focused in the right direction. All of our friends had given him the assignment of not letting me go down there and go off the grid. I must admit that I had made comments about that very act. After enduring the last few years, there is an urge to not only get away from it all, but an urge to totally withdraw from society, communication, or anything that might require me to make a decision, feel an emotion, or just generally act as if I cared about life. This feeling, I have been told, is normal, for a while. How long do I get to have these emotions? I don't know, but I still have some of them. This month's long trip, though, has at least divested me of the idea of becoming a hermit. I missed people too much, mostly my friends and their support. There exists this unseen force field. It is composed and bonded together by the love of people who take your personal well-being as their personal business. This force field is what holds the caregiver up when things get tough and go bad during the caregiving process; but it doesn't go away after the death of the loved one. It still exists and radiates over the caregiver as a buffer or cushion. It allowed me to continue on when everything else says, "Give up, and give in. I have lost. It is over." This force field, although unseen, is quite powerful and self-sustaining. The people who make up this force field know who they are; I don't have to mention them, but I will: Katie, Bennie, Julie, Ginger, Randy, Laura, The Disciples, The Cult, Harold, Judy, Beverly and many, many others. I could go on for chapters. The point is that I'm not alone. How selfish would it be if I ran off and became a hermit? These people put their souls into Kimberly's and my welfare. They never gave up on us and they have put up with my crap for so long. So while I feel alone, I know that I'm not. This is part of the transition in life that I must address.

There are so many new choices coming up in the near future. I sit on the tarmac in Miami waiting for the plane to taxi to DFW wondering: What am I going to do when I get there? What is the next step? What possibly could God have left for me to do? I literally have no direction, no focus, and honestly, no desire. I pray daily for God to send me a message or a sign. Please let me know what to do, what to look for. My last 33 years had focus and direction. I knew exactly what I was doing and where I was going, but now I'm a lost pup in the woods waiting for my master to send me a signal. What keeps me from giving up and giving in? My support group, that's who, and Kimberly. She told me before she died that if I didn't straighten up and fly right, she would haunt me big time. Not the Patrick Swayze and Demi Moore kind of haunting in _Ghost_, but the _Poltergeist_ kind. You know, where the unsuspecting victim gets sucked into the closet by a grinning, scary clown. That kind of haunting. Well, obviously,

I'm going to fly right. I have too many people who care about me. I would be letting them down if I didn't live right.

Now, what does all this have to do with transitioning through different levels of grief? Hopefully, to one day arrive on the other side as a healed person. Number one, I am not in this alone. Number two, I have responsibilities to people who love me to be the best I can be. Number three, at some point there always comes a crossroad. Every one faces them. That's life. Which road we take is important as this road decides future happiness and accomplishments. While going through the grieving process, the griever will reach points of choice. Places in time, different for each one of us, where, what we do takes us forward or backwards or, God forbid, downwards to destruction. These decisions are serious and can't be made lightly or with great emotion.

So, here I am. At my crossroad, at 31,000 feet (we finally took off), traveling west toward? I don't know, but the taking of this flight makes me wonder where I will land. Today, at DFW airport, tomorrow or the next day, still up in the air. I'm going to stop now, When I start this chapter back up I'll let you know which road I took.

❋

November 1, 2015, I spent Halloween with friends and their beautiful grandchildren. I watched the trick-or-treaters eagerly scurry around the neighborhood without a worry in the world. They were comfortable in the knowledge that a parent is a few feet away, and later they would fall asleep after coming down from the guaranteed sugar high. Last year, I wasn't very far from that same very spot with Kimberly by my side as we gave freshly popped popcorn to the kids. Then a participant, now a spectator, reminds me that transitions must take place at every level of life. I'm living in an apartment now on the edge of downtown, not in the suburbs where I spent all of my adult life to this point. To the view of many, I have made several transitions without much effort. Underneath the façade I am still spinning my wheels, searching for a direction to take. I'm still standing at the famously described crossroad waiting for a sign from God or at least an act that looks like it came from God. At this point I'd settle for a small sign, just something to help give me purpose and reason.

Next week is the six-month anniversary of Kimberly's death. Her beautiful black stone monument has been delivered and installed at her gravesite. The laser etched picture of the two of us in happier times is in the top left hand corner, a permanent record of our life together. The fresh green St. Augustine grass above her grave is already working its way through the Bermuda nearby. Someone visiting has left a golf ball and tee at the base perhaps in honor of the games they played together. I go by weekly to place fresh flowers and clean off the stone. Life goes on as, weekly, I see new stones being placed in the fairly new area of the cemetery. It is filling up quickly. Kimberly and I picked that spot out together when there wasn't much in this section of the cemetery, but a couple of graves in the area at the back corner. There are some beautiful shade trees nearby and a view of downtown only a couple feet away. The site is near where her grandparents are buried and very convenient for me living only a mile or two away.

Now, there are many new graves and stones dotting the hill. I see other loved ones with new grief on my weekly trips. I am obviously not alone in the world of those grieving. However, I often feel that way.

I have physically made the transition to living alone, but not emotionally. Kimberly and I always ate dinner together and watched our TV shows together, talking and laughing together as we discussed one plot or another. We spent 33 years as best friends, rarely apart. Now I eat my meals alone and watch TV without Kimberly's laughter. It is amazing how the desire for simple companionship grows so strong sometimes. It can be overpowering. I still do things with friends and other family members, but I'm talking about the intimate companionship of that special someone to whom I can tell my innermost thoughts, the one who understands me even when I don't talk, and the one who can finish most of my sentences if I do. She was the special one I could touch and hug and kiss whenever the desire came to me and she could do the same with me. This is definitely missing in my life and sometimes leaves me feeling very lonely.

Some might say it is time to transition to dating and finding a new companion, and there are times I consider it. But I know that it would be unfair to a person to attempt to date this soon. I am not ready yet. It is obvious to me. I have Kimberly's picture in many places in my bedroom and a video frame playing many pictures of us on trips we took in the last few years. There is a series of pictures that run together of us on the shore of Lake Tahoe, in front of a cabin in Fairbanks, Alaska, standing with Elvis in front of the Las Vegas sign, riding horses at the north end of the Big Island of Hawaii with Maui in the background, and my favorite, Kimberly and Katie pretending to be Greek Olympians at the sight of the original Olympics. Can you imagine bringing a date over to entertain with Kimberly's image appearing every few seconds? I know at some point it will be necessary to take away the pictures and the reminders. Maybe I will stop going to the gravesite every week, to just once a month, but not yet. As I have mentioned in an earlier chapter, the head, (practical,) and visual, (physical,) transitions occur sooner than the heart, (emotional,) transitions.

I have made progress that appears to outsiders that I am moving on. I ride a motorcycle and go hunting, two things that I did not do before. I can go to a restaurant, sit at the bar and order dinner by myself without going crazy. I can go to a party without a partner, sometimes--it is still hard to be at social gatherings. But many of these practices are done because I am making myself do them. There will come a time that I do them because I want to do them and enjoy them

Some transitions are natural and some transitions are things that happen with a great deal of effort and forced acts. As creatures of habit and comfort, we humans don't like change normally. It can be scary and stressful. When it is forced upon us, it can be downright petrifying. As I am in the middle of many transitions, I don't yet know the final outcome. I just know that I must keep going forward or I will most definitely go astray. I don't yet see the finish line but in the back of my mind, I know I'm in the final stretch and there is a checkered flag down that road somewhere. With the help of God, friends and family, I am not alone in the journey. Someday I will see the light and that light will show the way to the right crossroad to take, and that path will lead me to a new life. This new life will be completely different from the one I had planned with Kimberly, I know that, but to dwell on the what-ifs and the could-have-beens is a sad, lonely road that I refuse to travel.

So for now, I will force myself to get out of bed, make the bed, brush my teeth, and go do something useful or positive. My transitions will eventually lead me to another set of goals, new purposes, and, yes, possibly even a new companion.

❋

January 3, 2016, More than a month has passed since my last post on this topic. I now have two motorcycles and enjoy riding them as much as possible. Some people may think that not all my transitions are healthy for me.

I may agree, but not about the motorcycles. I love them and they give me a feeling of calmness and contentment when I go riding on a beautiful sunny day. Since this is a rare feeling, I will continue riding. I do understand the concerns of my loved ones who may think I have gone off the deep end. I had never in my previous 50 years owned or ridden much. This was mainly due to Kimberly having said, "Not, No. But Hell NO!"

I remember once back in the early nineties, I purchased a motorcycle from a friend on a whim. When I got home and began my wonderfully prepared speech for why I should get to keep it, it became very quickly apparent that it was going to be her or the bike. The bike was sold the next day. Kimberly was emphatic that if I was going to kill myself it was going to not happen on her watch while she still had a child to rear. It was hard to argue the point and I loved her and my daughter, so I gave up the folly. Later in my career, though, I was appointed the Commander of the Traffic Unit for the FWPD. As part of that command included the motorcycle unit, I could not pass up the opportunity to be trained on a large Harley Davidson Electra Glide. I loved the training and the ability to ride with pride and be a part of that unit for a few years. Kimberly couldn't stand it and let me know in no uncertain terms that if I got myself killed she would not let me hear the end of it. Having my best friend and police partner be a major motorcycle enthusiast, and never being able to go riding with him was very difficult. But I loved my wife more and when I left the Traffic Unit, I put aside the bike riding. But the love of the bike is there and will not go away.

So, a few months before she died, Kimberly told me she wanted me to buy a motorcycle.

Our daughter was married and gone off to Florida and there was no one left depending on me; therefore, I had her blessing. I didn't buy one though. There was too much going on and too many other worries. My heart would not be in it. I did appreciate that Kimberly wanted me happy when she left and she was willing to do anything to help ease my pain. It was a wonderful thought on her part. She also said she was ok with me going skydiving. She had forbidden that several years ago for the same reasons. I didn't do that either. For some reason, these things were no longer important or held any desire for me to do. I had other desires. A desire to spend every last minute with her and squeeze every last ounce of loving, compassionate, and blissful experiences with her that I could was all encompassing. But now she was gone. My transitional period continues.

My new life still awaits and the crossroads are still looming in forefront. I don't yet know where my life is going, but I know that I have to start living. The love of the motorcycle seemed a good start. The first bike, a 2004 HD Screaming Eagle CVO Deuce, was so beautiful and exactly what I had always wanted. I just had to have it. This bike though, is made for cruising and looking cool, loud and proud. It isn't really for long trips or heavy highway use. So, of course, I needed another bike to fit the need to travel, hence, the 2006 Honda Goldwing arrived. A beautiful traveler if there ever was one. I can't wait to take some long trips with friends. My transitions may seem a bit extreme from my past, but isn't that the point? My past is over and the future I had planned is not to be. I, therefore, must create a new future, doing things I love. I also have started a volunteer program. I work at the DFW airport as a volunteer ambassador, assisting travelers with directions and suggestions. It is very satisfying to help someone in need and stressed out, and there are lots of stressed out people at the airport.

I am getting used to living in the apartment near downtown, but to be honest I have only met one neighbor and have not attended any of the social functions that residents are invited to in the club house. It is still extremely hard to do social events with friends, but to do it with strangers seems downright crazy to me. Hopefully, that will change in the future but one day at a time.

I visit Kimberly's grave about every ten days. I clean the headstone and place new flowers. I go to a nearby movie theatre every other week and eat at local restaurants by myself. I sit at the bar and order dinner while watching the games on the big screens. These may seem like simple things, but to me they are completely different from the last 30 years and require some getting used to.

I have taken most of the pictures of Kimberly out of the living room, but keep a small memorial to her on a table next to my bed. I just can't seem to put them all away. There are days I feel so guilty even thinking of taking away reminders of her. Then there are days I chastise myself for dwelling on the past and staring at her picture, or reminiscing at old times. Transitioning to a new life isn't simple and often there are more steps backward than forward. There are good days, don't get me wrong. Days spent with friends or family or just riding my bikes for a few hours to clear my head. I take small trips and have several more planned in the near future. I know that I must continue to do things. My hope is that I will someday enjoy things as I had in the past. I'm not there yet, but it is getting a little easier. I also know that trying to serve others is a key to moving on with life. I continue to look for ways to best do that.

A short true story that recently occurred has helped me to see this also. My sister Laura had been dating a man for a couple months. They weren't very serious and still in the getting-to-know-each-other phase. He began feeling sickly and she went with him to the doctor. He was quickly diagnosed with cancer all over his liver. He told my sister that she better bail out now while the going was good. My sister, who had been through both our parent's bouts with cancer, and been a part of my struggle with Kimberly's illness, could have easily said her goodbyes and turned him over to relatives who would come from another state. She didn't though; she spent the next three weeks with him every day going to doctors and helping him with his rapidly declining health. It became obvious very quickly that matters were serious and he was not going to live. He died almost three weeks from diagnosis. My sister never left his side and even took leave from her job to take care of him. She told me she felt God had prepared her for that moment by all her past experiences. Her boyfriend had been alone in a new town with family far away. She never hesitated, but stepped forward and did what she could. She had taken adversity in her life, adversity that could have been debilitating, and turned it around to become strength. Instead of becoming self-serving, she became selfless. This was a lesson to me that you can't let your past suffering take you down and make you weak. Instead, you must use your experiences to help others. Toughness obtained from many hardships can be of use to others in their weak moments. I believe that God doesn't create bad things, but I do believe He helps us learn from them if we let him.

Part of transitioning to a new life is to realize that we are not the same person we were before, for better or worse. But the new person we become doesn't have to be broken and worn. We can make the choice to fight through the grief and see a better life ahead. We can choose to serve others and be happy again. Seven months after Kimberly's death, I'm not there yet, but I can see a little light.

✶

March 1, 2016, I am packing up the apartment, getting ready to move. Six months since first moving. It was a nice place, but city living is crowded, noisy and full of yuppies. There was no room for my stuff and I couldn't work on my motorcycles or cars in the garage. It just wasn't my thing. So, I chose a new path.

I purchased 5.6 acres out in the country. There is a ranch house and three perfectly fenced pastures. I plan to raise some calves on a very small scale, maybe a horse or goat or two, who knows. Quite a change from downtown city living, but hey, I have to keep moving in one direction or another. Hopefully, this move will settle me down at least for a few years and let me get some continuity in my life. I will be nearer to my best friend, Harold, and only a few miles further to my brother, Mike. Both of them have small ranches and can help teach me the ropes.

I enjoyed my volunteering at the airport, but it took only a little time. I still feel the need to accomplish more with my life. Working outdoors with animals on my own property seemed an ideal way to spend the days ahead.

Besides, there is a great Tex-Mex restaurant within two miles. I was sold. I have been lucky to get out of my rental lease with only a re-let fee. Someone wanted my apartment right away so I'll be moving out to the ranch, now called the "Rocking T2" after my dad's old brand. Mike's place is the "Rocking T," my dad's original old homestead where we were tended feeding pigs, cows, and horses. I will only be about ten miles from that place and somehow it feels natural to be returning near to some roots.

Sometimes transitioning to a new life can mean returning to an old one, a safe place, comfortable and secure. I honestly don't know if this will be my major crossroad that gets me over the hump or just another stop on a long journey to who knows where. All I really know at this point is that I'm moving forward in a positive way, with a few simple goals and some wonderful people nearby for support. I'll finish this chapter in a few months and give the reader a description of the move and the transition to rancher. It should be interesting, if I don't kill myself first. Until then I have a trip to the West Coast with friends!

❀

March 27, 2016, I moved into my new home almost two weeks ago and I love it out here. Peaceful, quiet, and slow just like I like it. I have a few goats already and have been working 12-hour days out in the pastures with fencing and mowing. There is something that happens when I sit on a tractor and just mow. My brain stops being busy and thinking too much, just relaxing and thinking about mowing. I spent several days just enjoying being outside with nothing but the tall grass for company. It was very calming and renewing. I am already sleeping better after tiring myself with many hours of good honest hard work. I am definitely learning a new trait that was never one of my strong suits—patience.

I don't think Kimberly would have ever moved out here. It is too quiet for her. But I do think she would have loved a small putting green next to the barn. She always wanted to be going and doing. I now feel comfortable and content to be working with nature and a bit of solitude. This transition appears to be working for me so far by keeping me busy while building something of my own. I will buy a few more goats and a couple longhorns, just enough to keep me busy. This is a different life than I had envisioned just a few years or months ago, but it is a good transition. I feel comfortable.

❋

May 1, 2016, I am but a week away from the anniversary of Kimberly's death. Since moving out to the country, I have worked from sun up to sun down, or as my friend, Harold, likes to say, "From can till can't." I have built fences, purchased cattle and goats, tended the land, and generally immersed myself into a different lifestyle than I could have envisioned only a few years before. As I end this chapter, I think I can answer Tanya Tucker's question, "What do I do with me?"

I keep living. I find things that interest me and make me content. At this point, after a long journey of grief and sadness, that is enough, for now. I have chosen to transition in to a completely new life that may or may not have pleased Kimberly if she were still here. At first that bothered me a bit, wondering if she would be pleased with my choices. But I have come to a place where I realize that we both are in different dimensions now and living separate existences. She is in Paradise and I'm out in the country as near to it as I can be. My transition is still on going and capable of change at a moment's notice but I feel a bit of calmness now that wasn't there before. I feel right in my direction and I sleep so much better. I have lost 15 pounds from hard work and getting the body back in some kind of shape after four years of sitting in waiting rooms under stressful conditions. Now my stress is related to keeping the goats out of the geraniums. Hard working at menial tasks is very conducive to healing, and like meditation, allows the brain to heal and think clearly once again. I enjoy sitting on my back porch with a glass of Tempranillo listening to music and watching Bonnie and Clyde, my longhorns, eat grass in the back pasture. I enjoy driving my tractor around mowing the tall grass grown after spring rains and listening to the goats as they complain that I'm not letting them out to eat it. I really enjoy the great Mexican restaurant, El Cerritos, 1.7 miles away. I eat there at least once a week with Harold and we just talk about farm stuff. These seem like simple pleasures to some. But to me, after a career of watching people suffer as a big city cop, and the love of my life suffer for so long, I am very content now for the simpler things in life. I have seen all the suffering I can handle. This feels like where I need to be.

I still plan to travel with friends as often as I can. That was one of the things Kimberly and I shared that will not go away, a legacy to her and her memory. I want to travel to so many places that she didn't see. Who knows where the future will send me.

"Living alone here in this place

I think of you and I'm not afraid

Your favorite records make me feel better

Cause you sing along

With every song

I know you didn't mean to give them to me

But you went away

How dare you?" [4]

[4] **"Over You" sung by Miranda Lambert-2011©
written by Miranda Lambert and Blake Shelton**

Chapter 9

Firsts

September 16, 2015, I want to talk about some firsts. Firsts start with the first day without the loved one and continue for infinity I guess. But during the first year after a death, there are many firsts such as first anniversary not celebrated, first birthday not achieved, or first holiday season not enjoyed. I have watched friends in the past go through these days and I could tell it was tough for them. Memories are fresh and the memories of recent celebrations that will no longer happen can make us dwell and regret with extra fervor.

My first, first? The first time I went to Kimberly's grave after her burial. I waited a week, due to exhaustion and extreme grief. I wanted to check on her flowers. There were so many wonderfully beautiful sets of flowers left on her newly sodded grave. When I arrived, it had rained heavily the night before; the new earth had sunk into the ground about six inches creating a bowl where the flowers had dropped down into the empty space. A couple of the standing arrangements had fallen over and all looked in disarray. I knew the workers would come by and fill the grave back to even now that the soil had settled, but I couldn't leave things as they were. I still felt the need to manage Kimberly's affairs. So I set about making things look good. I moved the flower arrangements around and fixed the standing arrangements firmly in the ground. They all still looked pretty good thanks to the rain. I loved the one with the golf theme. Kimberly's greatest love next to family and friends was golf. I now regret that I didn't take more interest in the sport. I tried for a while but I just didn't have the patience. Why couldn't I have tried harder for something she loved that much? I told her I would take it back up when we retired. Well I'm retired now, a little too late, huh?

I got the flowers back in shape and told myself I would come back each week and put new flowers on the grave. Her monument would take six more months to come in and a small flower arrangement would be the only acknowledgment that she was there for a while.

I thought back to her funeral and the steady rain that had begun falling just as the graveside service began and the sorrowful look on the faces of my good friends, as they slowly struggled to walk up the slick, grassy hill with Kimberly's casket. Truly the skies had opened up to cry with us as we laid her to rest. Katie and I dropped handfuls of earth into the grave; we walked away as the rain continued. Now, here a week later, the sun was shining. Kimberly's body was permanently laid at rest. Her soul was in Heaven, No more pain, no more suffering, and no more me. As I looked down at that sunken grave, I could only think, "Now what?" My first first only began a process that would continue, mockingly, unforgiving in its relentless journey of a year of firsts.

Now four months later, I have experienced my first trip alone, first July 4th weekend, and worst of all so far, our 31st wedding anniversary, which, technically didn't happen since I am now officially a widower. The emptiness that is experienced at these times is so much more than other days. It is expounded by memories from the past. We always tried to take trips for our major anniversaries. Last year was our 30th. Even though Kimberly was very sick and declining rapidly by this time, she insisted on one last trip; her last bucket list item. I took her on a cruise to the Baltic Sea. I was scared to death the whole time that she would need emergency care and I wouldn't find it when needed. But for her sake, I pretended I was fine. She pretended she wasn't in pain. Neither of us was very good at pretending. By this time, the tumors in her abdomen had grown to the point that pain was a daily occurrence. We had a lot of medication and used it. When she was feeling well, we did what she could. She was such a trouper in St Petersburg. For two days she walked all over and we took some wonderful pictures. In Copenhagen, she also did really well and we enjoyed a beautiful day looking at castles. But in Finland, we stayed onboard and only took a few small walks on the dock. In Stockholm, she insisted that I take our tour alone. It was a wonderful tour walking along the roof of the old Parliament building while receiving a talk about the history of the city. It was a beautiful, sunny day. She would have loved it. But she stayed on board and slept off some heavy meds. On August 18th, our official 30th anniversary, we made it to the fancy steak restaurant with window seats. As the waiter brought the wine menu, Kimberly became very sick and we returned to the room. We ordered sandwiches and spent the night in. She felt so bad about missing the dinner. But I was ok as long as she was ok. We knew this was our last anniversary together. We just wanted to be together and experience life as best we could.

We had several really good days after the cruise and Kimberly was able to travel by car to Bath, England. We had a wonderful time there. There were so many great memories to end with. The first day of sightseeing in Bath, she felt so well and was in such a good mood, that we walked all over the city and took pictures of everything possible. I was amazed at her energy as we strolled from one end of the city to the other, up and down hills and cobblestone streets. She never complained. Not once did she act as if she was putting on a good face for me. She was really enjoying herself, as if she knew the trip and her life-story would soon be over, and she must take it all in as best she could. There was a sense that all was coming to an end; we just didn't want to accept it yet. That day we lived.

Now these memories haunt my first anniversary without her. I sat alone in Costa Rica, watching the beautiful surf hit the beach, looking around to tell Kimberly to take a picture. She wasn't there of course. But I saw her many times. Sometimes it would be so surreal. I could sit there and look at an empty chair and imagine her sitting there relaxing and holding my hand. We would carry on a conversation. I could see it plainly as if it were real, I could imagine her every word and facial expressions. Is this what the firsts would be like, an imaginary experience of what ifs, a revisit of regrets, replays of past times that will never happen again? What will the seconds be like, I wonder?

After selling the house, I had moved into an apartment, my first home alone. I'm 51 years old and never lived alone for more than a few weeks. So here I am, slowly putting a home together by myself. I got a new, smaller bed. I changed out a few pieces of furniture but by and large I am using all the things that we had in our old home. Dealing with family portraits was a tough one. Kimberly told me not to hang all of our old pictures of us two together; that I would need to move on and not dwell every day on her. The problem is that everything reminds me of her. It doesn't have to be a picture of her. Every song that has been recorded since 1981 reminds me of her. Every movie made since our first date in December of 1981, where we saw <u>Raiders of the Lost Ark</u> on opening night, reminds me of her. Every restaurant, every-everything reminds me of her. So there was no way I was going to Kimberly proof this apartment. I did the best I could to find the right balance between memory and shrine. When the time is right, these pics can be changed out easily with new pictures and new memories. I don't know when that time will be. There are still too many firsts to come. The holidays are coming soon.

Kimberly loved decorating for fall, Halloween, and Christmas. She loved spending time with family and friends during this time of the year. She loved entertaining friends and playing games. She was in her element when playing any game with large groups of people; and, boy, did she like to win.

So I have to go through this first over the next few months without her. I always imagine her in these situations, as if a ghost were still there in the chair playing along, laughing, and loving her friends. I feel half a person in these situations now. I pretend to be my old self, but I'm not. I never will be because Kimberly will always be the missing piece of me. People who lose a limb to sudden tragic accidents often say they have feelings of a ghost limb for many years afterward. A feeling of phantom pain or movement as if the limb was never gone. That is what I feel every day. My main limb is missing. My soul feels her presence when I wake in the morning and when I lay down at night. As I go through each day, I see her everywhere and talk to her often. She still guides many of my moves and is part of my conscious. I don't just ask myself, "What should I do?" But, "What would Kimberly want me to do?" Sometimes I get blessed with a dream where she still lives and we talk and hug. I awake in the morning to reality and cry. All I want to do is go back to sleep, find that dream again and stay there forever.

How do I start fresh a new life when the old life that was ripped away from me keeps rising up? I tried running away. It doesn't help. I am haunted by wonderful memories of a wonderful life. Thirty years of blessings, goals achieved together with a partner playing on the same sheet of music. Now I live in a world that seems strange and I am out of sync with my surroundings. Every "first" acts as an adrenaline shot to intensify these feelings. By the time one ends, another begins.

Kimberly's 51st birthday is next week. I am going out of town with friends to make a new memory. Will this help or will the haunting memories follow me? Then what of the holidays?

※

October 7, 2015, I'm returning home from a wonderful trip with friends, on the road with my thoughts and remembrances. Big Cedar in Missouri and Nashville, Tennessee are both places I have spent time with Kimberly and have so many memories as I revisit these places. A new set of "firsts" continues. Each occurrence where I repeat an activity once completed with Kimberly, now experienced alone takes an effort, but must be experienced. It is part of the healing that makes me do these things. Somehow my brain feels the need to paste over the old memories with new ones that don't include her. It seems mean in a way, as if I am erasing her out of my life or pretending she wasn't the most influential human for all those years of my life, but it is the only way to pave the future. I can't always walk with her ghost at every experience. There has to be new experiences and new memories built that don't include her. I almost feel I am betraying her as I write this, but I know it's true, so I go forward. I pave over the old memories and create the new with good friends. Next year will be easier, right? The second time is always easier, right?

Halfway through this trip, I got a call that Kimberly's stone monument for her gravesite was ready and they were laying it the next day. I had planned to be there. I don't know why really, I guess just part of my anal nature to stay in control. That didn't work either. Anyway, Kimberly's mother and aunt were there and took some great photos of the installment and the final look with some new red roses ensconced in the granite vase. It is beautiful. I designed the monument and Kimberly approved the final draft. I know she would be pleased. This first, the first time I saw the name of my love carved in stone with the date of death, that's tough. I stared at the pictures for some time trying to come to grips with the finality of it. The only thing I can think of as I stare at the carved letters and the phrase, "Till the twelfth of never" (Our song) with musical notes for quotes, is that there is no dash between the dates. I realize that the dash is the most important part of the stone, because that is where her life was lived, between the dates. That dash is so small a thing but contains every wonderful action of a wonderful life well lived. That dash contains a little over half a century of life lived and 33 years of it with me. I am so lucky to have been given that gift. I just didn't want to give it back. Maybe I can add the dash to the monument at a later date.

Kimberly's headstone a few days after deliver;
a visitor had left a golf ball and T.

January 4, 2016, my "first" Christmas season and New Year celebration without Kimberly has come and gone. I spent Christmas with my daughter, Katie, and my son-in-law, Will, skiing in Breckenridge, Colorado. This was a favorite of Kimberly's and Breck has always been our ski town of choice. As we enjoyed the Christmas week, we continued with many of the same old traditions from the past. We put up the same small tree with the colorful LED lights; we put up the same stockings that were handmade by Kimberly's mother, minus Kimberly's of course. We ate at many of the same old restaurants that we had grown to love. The one tradition that both Katie and I saw as a must, was waiting in line in the freezing cold weather to get a homemade crepe' from The Crepe' Shoppe, a small kiosk on the street that always had a line no matter what season. This was one of

Kimberly's favorite places and we knew she was with us in the cold, having a good laugh watching us freeze for tradition's sake. All of this was new for Will, my new son-in-law. Katie and I enjoyed including him in the old traditions. We also added some new traditions that I'm sure will be practiced in the future. After receiving our piping hot crepes, we ran down to a little place we had found the day before called, Apres. It had the most wonderful mixture of hot drinks and whiskeys. Full of colorful locals and friendly people, we grabbed a board game off the shelf and played all day. As a special bonus, it was right next door to another tradition, the homemade bakery that specialized in making cookie sandwiches. Who would ever need to leave that spot? The three of us played Yahtzee and drank hot brandies and whiskeys for several of the days when not skiing. We also continued an old tradition of watching Christmas movies such as <u>Christmas Vacation</u>, and <u>Christmas Story</u>. We had done that for years, but this year we added a new movie to our repertoire, <u>Bull Durham</u>. The reader might be thinking, "That isn't a Christmas movie; it is a baseball movie." True, but we had so much fun watching the movie and enjoying our time together, Will and I decided it would definitely become part of the tradition. On Christmas Eve, we ate at a new restaurant, where we had bison tenderloins. The meal was delicious. Our old place had closed due to the owner retiring. So, we had a good mix of old and new. I do believe this was a very good way to experience a "first." The old traditions felt comfortable and a tribute to Kimberly's memory; whereas, the new felt fresh and fun when adding a new person to our group. New experiences were shared together and old traditions were taught and explained. It just felt right. I will admit there were moments of sadness and melancholy. It couldn't be avoided. But there was also a feeling of taking a step forward into a new life for Katie and me.

My New Year's Eve was spent at the lake with my friends where we have trailers in a fishing park on Lake Fork. The food is always awesome and the comradery and East Texas kindness can't be beat. Although this is not where Kimberly and I had spent past New Year's Eve, it was one of our go-to places and there are many memories there. But the New Year's celebration was new. The decks were all decorated with lights and heaters and fires were burning everywhere to keep the deck warm for dancing. I always feel welcome there and when surrounded by friends who care, it is hard to be sad. However, again, melancholy set in and became my partner.

I do think this will be the norm for some time. As Chapter 8 illustrated, transitions are hard to complete. They really are long-term processes and not one time events. One or two steps forward and one or two steps back are normal. These "firsts" are repeats of special events and occurrences that once were taken for granted. I just always assumed they would be spent each year with Kimberly as the years rolled by. Now I see that each one of them in the past was in themselves special in its own right and should have been treasured intently at the time, with the knowledge that they would never be repeated again.

So, now here I am, trying to make new special events, with new and old mixed together to create a new "special." I have a few more "firsts" to go before the "seconds" start. Valentine's Day, my birthday, and Mother's Day--this will be especially hard on Katie. I will continue to try and blend the old with the new and make new memories. It seems the best way to go.

❋

February 21, 2016, I have now experienced Valentine's Day as a widower, a new first. I stayed home and played Grand Theft Auto Five and ate spaghetti. At least, I saved a hundred bucks on flowers. Kimberly, as most women do, loved Valentine's Day. She would always put red stickers all over our mirror with hearts and "I Love You"'s all around. We learned to eat out the night before or after due to the giant crowds and lousy service on the actual day. I can't say that I missed celebrating Valentine's Day per se, but I do miss celebrating anything with Kimberly. It came and went as fast as it could, thank goodness.

My first birthday without Kimberly, yesterday, was another thing. I think my friends wanted me to be busy so they had a full day planned. We spent the morning touring my new ranch. I move in soon, and then had an afternoon tour and a few tastings at a local winery. That night, we went out to dinner at one of my favorite restaurants. I love my friends and the effort they take in making me feel special and included. We were a group of six couples and are now a group of four couples and two widow/ers. The road goes on forever and the party never ends. (Thanks Mr. Keen).

As I discussed earlier, I bought a small ranch. Moving in to the apartment was my first place alone, and it had been quite a transition. Now I have a small five-acre ranch out in the country, alone. This place is to keep me busy with my new way of life, a life I'm still fleshing out and trying to define. It seems to be more of a transition topic than a "first." but being my first second, I felt the need to mention it here.

❀

March 8, 2016, Ten months now have passed after Kimberly's death. A few more firsts to go then some dates begin to repeat. Other occurrences, unexpected and new to me will still be firsts, but over time will become just that, new experiences and not "firsts." My melancholy moods still occur. I still have bouts of depression and self-pity. I still play the what-if game from time to time, and I still have wonderful dreams that Kimberly lives in. Dreams I hope never stop, or should I not hope that? I don't really know. There is still a large part of me that doesn't want to let go and a part that knows I will have to find a place to put my good memories and let them just be memories. I think I see a light up ahead, maybe, I'm not sure but maybe it's a light.

❋

April 28, 2016, the five year anniversary of Kimberly's diagnosis was six days ago. A day that changed the rest of my life and an anniversary that I thought I would never forget. Yet, I didn't think about it until today. On April 22, I was out in the back pasture working on a barn door. I didn't even think of the date. I'm not sure if this is progress or I was just too busy to notice. Maybe it was both. Maybe this "first" is the first time I wasn't directly affected by a date in time or a memory of the past because I was busy living. I will always remember that day. It is burned into my mind like many others, but is it possible that I'm getting past this phase of grief and moving on? Is this healing? I hope so, I really do. There is no way to recover (heal, transition?) from a long period of suffering and grieving without putting away some of the bad memories in the back of my mind and letting the good memories come forward.

As of today, I still dwell on things but not as often. I still do the "What if" game, but not as much as before. I go days now without sad thoughts or regretful feelings. I look forward to the next day and what I can accomplish. These are positive actions and recent firsts for me. The first time I felt normal for a while is a new one for me.

Next week is the last first, the first anniversary of Kimberly's death. Update coming. Stand by.

✳

May 8, 2016. One year after Kimberly's death. Also Mother's Day. My last first? Katie and Will were in town and we met family near her resting place for breakfast and then went to the graveside with pink roses. The first year after is over. Being on Mother's Day, it was extra melancholy for Katie and her Grandmother, Bennie. It was slowly raining, very similar to the day we buried her as we laid the flowers in the vase. But unlike that day, the sun began to shine just a bit as we drove away.

This picture was taken one year after Kimberly's death, May 8, 2016. Pictured is Myself, my daughter, Katie, son-in-law, Will, and mother-in-law, Bennie.

I don't visit the gravesite as much as I did, about once a month or a special date, like this day. That is normal also, though and I know that Kimberly is not there really. It is only the remains of a part of us that we are never meant to keep for long. I will be there beside her someday and others can visit us together and share memories of times we spent together. Eventually the visits will only be for the special dates like her birthday and our anniversary. The firsts are over now and the seconds begin. I think they will be easier. I'm always full of fond memories and less of grief and suffering. As my life moves forward I'm learning to cope and deal with memories in a better fashion. I loved my life with Kimberly and will always cherish the time we had together and the memories will always be in the back of my mind. But now, I move forward, on toward new firsts. I know there will still be tough times. Three hundred and sixty-five days is not the perfect timeframe for grieving and recovery, but somehow it seems like a page gets turned and a new chapter starts as the next year begins. My grieving in some ways continues, but I am not suffering and there has been much healing. That is progress.

"Oh yea, life goes on

Long after the thrill of livin' is gone ..." [5]

---

[5] **"Jack and Diane" sung and written by John Cougar Mellencamp 1982©**

Chapter 10

Finding the New Normal

December 1, 2015. Some people say that life is a roller coaster ride, full of ups and downs. But it isn't really. A roller coaster ride ends after the thrill, but life must goes on. (Thanks, Mr. Mellencamp.)

As I begin this chapter, I am still completing chapters eight and nine. But in addressing those topics, I must also begin to look at what is beginning to look normal for me. Now that I am cooking one-person meals, I have noticed something that gave me thought. Have you every cut a fresh avocado in half; pulled the parts away and eaten one half and stored the other half in the fridge for the next meal? Then, when you pull that other half out of the fridge, it has turned partially black and a little softer than the first half was the day before. So, you cut away the black and soft parts and make do with what you have left. Well, that is what I have had to do with my life; cut away the black parts and try to make do. The black parts were representing the anger and other negative feelings that have controlled much of my life for many months. You see, I wanted the fresh first part of the avocado to last forever. Well, life goes on doesn't it? Now I must make do with what I can salvage; or do I?

What do I see as the new David? The old David was happily married and resting on his laurels somewhat. I would be content to move on to an early retirement and travel in my fifth-wheel around America with my wife. We would spend our later years on travel and leisure. That normal is gone now. So, what is the new normal to look like? Since I am early in this chapter and only seven months from Kimberly's death, I will start by saying much of the new normal sucks.

There are days and mostly nights where the loneliness and desire for intimate contact are excruciating. Now when I say intimate contact, I don't necessarily mean sexual contact. That is normal in any red-blooded American 51-year-old, but what I'm talking about is the ability to sit and talk and/or snuggle with someone who knows my every nuance. To be in the same room with someone who I know to be mine and mine alone, whose unconditional love exudes from her like a perfume that only I can smell. This person takes away loneliness with a smile, or a soft look, or a small touch. I miss that so much. This is at the present the new normal.

But I know that it doesn't have to always be this way. That is to be determined. It is obvious to me that there are a lot of lonely people in a world full of people. I didn't see it before, but I see it now. When I go to the grocery store, I witness the couple together shopping and laughing and enjoying their time together, or like Kimberly and me, fighting over what to buy. Then I see the single person who one can tell is alone by what they pull off the shelf. Try it sometime when you go to the grocery store. Try a weekday when it isn't too crowded, and try not to look like a stalker. But watch what a single person buys and the small packaging he or she use. Did they get the quart of juice or the gallon? Do they only shop for men's products or is a man in the woman's aisle getting his wife her personal stuff? It is amazing what you observe when you find yourself living another sort of life.

So, it is already apparent to me that I do not want to be a hermit, living alone and buying a pint of milk, half loaf of bread, and the small carton of Blue Bell Ice Cream. I want a companion. Someone who sends me to the store to buy her the dark brown eye liner, even though she knows I'll never find it. That normal is a ways off though, back to my present normal. I ride my motorcycles twice a week at least. I enjoy that immensely and will never stop. I go to movies by myself and have learned to eat at the bar. I am often the third or fifth wheel with my friends, but they don't seem to mind. I am constantly looking for ways to be useful in my life, and sometimes I have days that I feel successful and fulfilled and some days where I feel useless and have wasted the whole day. I have curbed my alcohol use back down to my norm of two drinks a day--mostly. Some days are better than others in that area, but I'm getting better. Remember, I'm a work in progress. It is plain to me though that I must get busy moving forward, or I will definitely slip backward.

As my grieving process continues, life still goes on. Others are experiencing their own problems and issues and need help. A person can't afford to selfishly stay a basketcase forever, while others are in need. I will continue looking for a place that is normal in my life where I feel I am contributing to society. Until then, I try to keep looking forward, blending old and new, waiting for the Lord to open a door for me.

❋

March 27, 2016, Easter Sunday, I got up this morning at 7:30, made coffee and sat on the back porch and read the resurrection story out of Matthew. I had my own little sunrise service. My brother and sister came out and we went to lunch. Is this a new normal for my Easter? Perhaps, but it felt right for now. <u>Normal</u> is a very relative word. What is normal for me may not be normal for someone else. I guess normal is when a person feels good about what he is doing on a day-to-day basis and is happy with his life as it is. I haven't had that for quite some time, so there was no normal. Now I'm beginning to feel pieces of normal creeping in to my life. My wake up and morning routine is becoming at least familiar. I get up around 7:30, make coffee, and open all the shades in the house to let in the sun. I can do that in the country when my house is far enough away from the next house. Then, I make breakfast while I read the news on my iPAD. Then, out to work in the pastures. I'm trying to get my back pasture ready for a couple Longhorn cattle. I have a good long day outside working and then in for the evening. Some days I visit with friends who live nearby or a dinner at a local restaurant. It is starting to feel comfortable.

As I set up my new home, I continue to blend my old furnishings with new ones that fit my new ranch house look. I am creating the new me from pieces of the old me and new ideas for the future. It is working with my house and with my goals and ideas of what the future will be for me. I am still evolving, but I am definitely moving in a direction I feel good about. That is a good start.

❈

May 1, 2016. Katie and Will are coming in next week for a few days and I am really excited to have them out here to the new place, my new normal. I've got the house just about the way I want. I have been fixing the upstairs room as a guest room for them to stay. Old pictures of family are on the walls as well as places we have been. Hopefully, Katie will feel at home. It is quite different than the place she left after she got married and moved to Florida, but I want her to feel that it is her second home at any and all times. I know that she has been apprehensive about leaving me for her new life. It is important that she sees that I'm ok, that I'm going to make it. Katie and Will have created a great home for themselves in Florida and they seem very happy. It is a place that I can go visit easily and hang at the beach with family. I'm very happy and excited to watch their future unfold. It reminds me of my early marriage. We were full of plans and ideas, and we achieved many of our goals together. It was a great 30 years. I wish much more for them. Their normal is now Florida, but that could change. Life has a way of doing that to a person, changing on a dime, I mean.

A very dear friend of mine, Melissa, was married for over 30 years. She and John had two wonderful adult children and a beautiful grandchild. They had purchased a yacht that they planned to one day move to Florida and live out their retirement dreams. A perfect marriage, a perfect set of goals and dreams were changed on a dime. John died in his sleep from a pulmonary embolism. They had just had a wonderful dinner together, and gone to bed thinking the next day would be the same normal day. Now, like me, Melissa has had to build a new normal. The yacht is sold and the Florida retirement cancelled. Melissa still struggles almost two years later as she still builds her "new" normal. We talk often about the differences in our spouses' deaths.

Her situation with John was unexpected and sudden. There was no suffering, only immediate shock and disbelief. Also, she also had no ability to say goodbye, make plans, or fulfill a bucket list together. Her grief only began the day of his death, but continues due to the unbelievable shock. John's last checkup had showed he was in perfect health for a 59-year-old-man. There were no signs of what was too come.

I, on the other hand, had my initial shock in 2011 and had years to suffer and grieve with Kimberly as she went through the process of treatment--only to end in a sure death. We completed a bucket list, made plans, and said goodbye. There was nothing left to be done in the end but kiss her goodbye. Which way to go, you ask? Melissa and I talked about this and neither can say. We just have our individual experiences and grieve as a loved one does. We both have tried to create our new normal.

I have been more radical while Melissa has changed very little of her life. She still works at a job she loves and still travels to visit her granddaughter whenever she can. We both still travel with our friend group but now she and I get our own little studio suite rooms. The 12 have become 10. That is the new normal. Maybe John and Kimberly talk together and enjoy stories of the past. I surely hope so.

Comparing my experiences with Melissa's have been interesting in that we both lost our spouses, but under extremely different circumstances. We both have grieved and continue to live. But we both have had to create a new normal in our lives in order to move forward and make an attempt at happiness. She has kept many things the same and I have made many things different, and yet there are many similarities to our situations. First, we both couldn't have survived without our faith. It is imperative that a person believe in something or someone greater than oneself. The need for hope, grace, and mercy from a greater power is immense. I have had days when only my belief in God kept me from making a very bad decision to end my own life. Only the knowledge that I was placed on this earth by God as a gift of love and taking it away would be an unforgiveable sin kept me from the deed. That is the nature of grief as it overcomes the strong and the weak alike. We all need something to hang on to that makes us more than we are alone. The reader may not be a believer in God, but one needs to believe in something bigger to survive the overwhelming loss of a beloved spouse.

Secondly, Melissa and I share a group of friends and families that surrounded us like bullet-proof vests. Our support structure was such that we were never in want. I cannot imagine trying to go through this struggle alone. Our new normal will always included these people and the Good Lord, even as we change into our new, future selves.

My normal life now is slower and predicable, working a small ranch by myself and trying to grow it slowly is a lot of work, with long hours outside in the sun and working fences and livestock. I actually look forward to the next day and accomplishing something. Something I consider important and fulfilling that may not be considered thrilling to some but is satisfying to me. This is a good start only one year out from the lowest point in my life, a time when only clouds hung over me and gloom and suffering was all around. I still have a ways to go as I realize that I will never stop grieving really, you just get use to the empty space in your heart. You learn to live with it and still look for the sun. As I change to a new future, I will remember a wonderful past as a former life lived and moved on to another. I will not dwell and sulk any longer. When I remember, it will be with love and fondness for the past but also with a longing for a brighter future. Hopefully, I will be wiser and have more compassion for others as I try to help those who have helped me, because I know that life will continue to give us changes whether they are quick like Melissa's or long like mine. Either way there will be grief and the grieving need to be surrounded by loved ones.

Back for a moment to my avocado analogy, the question is do I make do with the mushy second half from the day before, or do I throw it out and get a new avocado? For me, I just can't see being happy for the next stage of my life clinging to old regrets and habits that keep me "making do." I feel the need to re-invent my life to be something completely different not because the past was bad or wrong, but because it was with Kimberly and our lives were intertwined. All of our decisions were together and for each other. Now, there is just me trying to make me happy. I can blend what I liked from the past and add these things to my future life creating a whole new person if I want. I think the key is figuring out what to keep and what to carve away. If I am still making do, then I need to keep carving away. When I am living happily and satisfied where I am, then I have the new me, and ultimately a new avocado. So, the new normal is a changing thing that will evolve over time and a great deal of effort.

Today's normal gets worked like a fresh clay pot on a wheel, until finally it becomes the work of art I want it to be. When I get my normal where I am content with my life then I can look forward once again to seeing life with gusto and eager to see tomorrow. I believe the worst thing I could do to Kimberly's memory is stay satisfied with the idea that I really don't care whether I live or die today. I want to wake up each morning, thanking God that he gave me another day to live, even if it is just to eat a fresh avocado.

Chapter 11

A Year in Retrospect

May 8, 2016. Kimberly died 365 days ago and was buried on a cold, rainy day a few days later. Today ... a cool rainy day also, but a hint of sun was on the horizon.

A couple days ago we had a big BBQ picnic at my new place in the country. All of the people who have surrounded me and my family the last several years were there except a few dealing with their own family issues. The day was picture perfect, not a cloud in the sky with temperature in the upper 70's. My two cows posed for pictures as my goats cried out for attention from the children. My friends and family laughed and played games as we ate fresh smoked beef, venison, pork, and chicken. My brother's beer chicken was by far the best. Katie and Will were in town and it was a very good day! The symbolism was everywhere, new babies, new spring flowers, new beginnings abound.

Unfortunately, with a book about grieving, it is hard to have a happy ending; however, my goal is to leave the reader with a light to stretch toward, a direction or path that might be obtainable. I have not mentioned many other sufferings that have occurred in the last year with people I know and love. Friends have been diagnosed with cancers and other diseases, some have also lost loved ones, others are close to the end of their lives, and still others struggle with inner demons that make life very complicated. But there have also been many new births of children, new jobs and promotions, and new marriages bringing together new families. In other words, life didn't stop while I was grieving. The world has continued to turn and stuff will continue to happen. It is time now for me to get back into it and see what I can do to help. Maybe be there for someone else like they were for me. It is time. This last year has been a time of change and reflection, of inner searches for meaning and outward struggles to maintain a normal feel for life. People have been very patient with me while I have struggled through my metamorphosis. In the old days, when a spouse died, widows donned all black and shunned public appearances for one year in a sign of grievance. Then, once the year was up, they immediately changed into new colorful clothing and were often expected to remarry right away. This was the way, with no real thought into the person's honest feelings or inner struggles. How they came up with a year's time, I don't know for sure but it many ways it seems logical to me. As I documented in the chapter on firsts, that first year is not unlike the course from the <u>American Gladiator</u> TV show. There is one set of hurdles after another, each one taking a bit out of the athlete, slowly draining his strength and will to continue. Many don't make it through to the end. There was always something to trip them up. But, for those few who did make it to the final button, a sense of accomplishment and a vanquished foe exists.

That first year of grief was like that and to make it over that hump has left me with a sense of getting to the next phase of life. A year doesn't end the struggle and change everything. Many people take much longer, as it was with Melissa and her loss of John so suddenly. Circumstances abound that make each situation so much different, however, as has been said many times in many ways, time does tend to help heal wounds. It allows for thought and contemplation, for perspective and reflection, and lastly, time gives us a chance, if we take it, to heal and move forward.

I have read many books on the topic of grief and grieving and have always been left wanting more. The more is, of course, the wonderful ending where everything has finally gone well and the world looks like opportunity again. I must admit that this is a daunting task. One year does not provide, not in my case, at least, that type of ending. There is just too much baggage left to sort. I must say that I continue to persevere, sometimes by sheer will alone. But, I think that is the point. I must have a will to survive, to overcome, and to adapt. A human spirit exists in us all that says, I can do it, I can make this hurdle, and I will not succumb to life's sorrows. If I had this attitude in my life before the tragedy occurred, then, when it does, my programming can kick in and I can get through the rough times. Grief and suffering is neither for the weak at heart, nor for the quitter when life gets tough. I have found solace in true story novels and movies about people that have made it through Hell and survived. A recent movie, <u>Unbroken</u>, about a WWII hero, that survived years in a Japanese prison camp and became a great voice for God and country is one example. My plight seems so small next to these true stories. Surely, I can put forth the effort to survive and be an active, positive force in my world. I'm not saying it will be easy or that the days will become like days at the beach with sunshine and butterflies, but they can be productive to those around me in need of my experience and hard-earned wisdom.

While we heal we can become the wise word needed by someone else just beginning a bad journey. It is my belief that the path back to normalcy has to go through self-sacrifice and service to my fellow man. It is hard to wallow in my own self-pity when I am busy keeping someone else afloat who is afraid of drowning. Remember the movie, It's a Wonderful Life? George Bailey was about to commit suicide but did not hesitate to jump in the freezing river to save another man whom he thought was trying to do exactly what he contemplated seconds before. A good person will always stay a good person no matter the situation going on around them if he or she can fight off the anger and bitterness that may overcome their better self. If we concentrate our efforts to those more in need than we are, we become fulfilled again. We can lose the feeling of total uselessness and lack of purpose that keeps us depressed. I spent four years with the very important job as caregiver for Kimberly. When she died, I was not only jobless, but felt like a failure because I did not stop her death from occurring. I had no purpose or reason left to be a productive person in my community. The first goal was to forgive myself, then to start setting new goals that I could work toward. Never give in to the desire to quit and give up. Fight through the negative mind sets that control my quiet moments. If I can find the right path, I can reset my life, find a new purposeful reason for living, and even maybe someday find a new love with whom to share this path. I don't share these insights as accomplishments I have already achieved, but as goals and visions I have placed before myself. Some might call it the light at the end of the tunnel, to have a direction to walk toward. Perhaps it is and perhaps it isn't, but it is a direction.

Today, I will choose to be satisfied with a direction. That is called, "taking a step".

We have to learn to walk again, yes?

Reflections

I hope this story of my struggle with grief helps someone who may feel alone in the world. We are never alone. All we need do in most cases is reach out a hand and allow someone to grasp it. If you are reading this book because you have recently begun a struggle with grief, please reach out. Do not go alone down this path. Find something to hang on to and let your self be lifted. I was completely without hope and lost to the world. I did not believe in a future or have any desire for one. Now I'm on a farm raising goats and cows. Who knew? There are so many who want to help, just make a cry. This small book is but a year in my life of many years, and my hope is that the future will look bright again as new chapters are written. I have been told that this story is really two stories; one is a love story and the other a story of grief. I agree. This is my last love letter to Kimberly. I use to write her many of them when I was away in the military or off to school. She kept them all. This last love letter she will have to read in her own way. I hope I loved her enough and said the words often enough. She always said I did, but wanted to hear it again anyway. She knew I would grieve for her and it hurt her to know it was coming. This book is my way of telling her it will be ok, I will be ok.

If the reader wants to know what occurred in time after the year described above, I will update Kimberly's Caringbridge.com account. Look for the update by May 8, 2017@ CaringBridge.org/visit/kimberlyingram.™

Special Thanks

Thank you to my dear friend, Laura Blalock who allowed me to use her as a sounding board throughout this process. Thanks to my editor, Shelley Cook, who not only dealt with many grammar issues but also understood what I was trying to do and helped me get there. Special thanks to Katie, my daughter, who always is there with support and encouragement. And lastly, thanks to my friends and family who make my life worthy.

About the Author

David W. Ingram is a retired 25-year veteran of the Fort Worth, Texas Police Department. A Texas native and graduate of Midwestern State University, David retired from policing to become a full time caregiver to his wife, Kimberly, of 30 years. David now owns and manages a small ranch in Springtown, Texas just miles from the farm where he grew up.

2/10/17

Made in the USA
Lexington, KY
04 February 2017